To the Reader:

It is a pleasure and a privilege for Black Ministry of The Lutheran Church—Missouri Synod, in partnership with Concordia Publishing House, to bring to you some classic books about the history of LCMS Black Ministry.

This year, we are thanking God for 140 years of black ministry in our church. These resources are intended to help you understand the history of black ministry in the LCMS and to help you grow in your appreciation for the work of our forefathers and foremothers on whose shoulders LCMS Black Ministry was launched. These resources tell the history of Sunday School classes, Christian school education, and Word-and-Sacrament congregations gathered around the historic confessions of the Lutheran Reformation: grace, faith, and Scripture in Christ—to the glory of God alone! It is the history of how the Gospel message changed the lives of untold thousands of black Americans only fourteen years from enslavement and thirty years from the founding of the LCMS. It is a history of great joy and immense struggles, as black Lutherans celebrated their heritage as Lutherans and stood up for their Lutheran equality and inclusion.

As this early mission work unfolded, the narrative was recorded in the verbiage and language of the time. These resources are the written history of those who lived in a segregated, prejudiced, and xenophobic society, especially in the Deep South, where most of LCMS Black Ministry started before spreading throughout the United States.

Neither I nor Concordia Publishing House endorse, embrace, or approve of such language. But we discussed the historic nature of the works and are reproducing these resources in the language of the writers. As the leader of LCMS Black Ministry, I asked Concordia Publishing House to make these books available again. My prayer is that you find in these books the historic narrative of a great number of Lutheran pastors, educators, and laypeople who left us the legacy of black Lutheranism, rich in its heritage.

We stand on the shoulders of those courageous, faithful men and women who have preserved our faith and heritage as Lutherans. They have left us a legacy that we must courageously fulfill for the future, for new generations of laypeople, educators, deaconesses, pastors, and other church workers for centuries to come—to witness of the glorious Gospel of our Savior, Jesus Christ, God's salvation for everyone who believes it.

As we look back 500 years to the start of the Reformation and at 140 years of LCMS Black Ministry, we can see we are at the threshold of a Reformation for these new generations to come. Like Drs. Rosa Young, Robert King, Richard Dickinson, Julius Jenkins, and others, we have a mission to accomplish. May God gift us with His Spirit to faithfully engage the world with His love, mercy, and grace in Christ.

Now, "may the God of hope fill you with all joy and peace in believing, so that by the power of the Holy Spirit you may abound in hope" (Romans 15:13).

Sincerely, serving Christ and His Church,

Rev. Dr. Roosevelt Gray Jr.
Director, Black Ministry
LCMS Office of National Mission

June 7, 2017

Half a Century

of

Lutheranism

Among Our Colored People

A JUBILEE BOOK

by

CHRISTOPHER F. DREWES

DIRECTOR OF MISSIONS

1877—1927

ST. LOUIS, MO.

CONCORDIA PUBLISHING HOUSE PRINT

1927

FOREWORD.

Our Colored Missions are this year celebrating their Golden Anniversary. This fact in itself justifies the publication of this book. We are sure that every friend of our Negro Missions would have been disappointed if our Board for Colored Missions had permitted this year of jubilee to go by without putting forth a record of the wonderful blessings God has poured out upon our Church's humble labors among the freedmen during the past half-century.

The Board was most fortunate in its selection of the writer of this record of God's grace and blessings. No man living possibly could have been so fitted to write a history of our Negro Missions as its Director, the Rev. C. F. Drewes. Having been a member of the Mission Board since 1908, its chairman from 1911 to 1916, and the Director of our Negro Missions for the past ten years, who else could have been found that had so much first-hand knowledge of this missionary enterprise?

To this knowledge must be added, in the case of Director Drewes, an interest in the work and a conviction of its importance such as few others can have, and the ability to tell the whole story of God's gracious dealings in a most simple, natural, straightforward, and, withal, gripping way. The writer of these lines read almost the whole book at one sitting. He would have finished it at one reading had he not been obliged to hurry to the railroad station to catch a train. Once safely seated in the train, he finished the remaining pages, only regretting that there were not more left to be read. —

Not a small share of the burden of carrying on the enterprise has rested on Director Drewes for almost two decades, that period which saw the most rapid growth and widest expansion of the work. Often was he called upon to find solutions for problems that would have tested the faith, patience, and courage of the greatest and bravest. His guidance and inspiration are everywhere apparent upon the extended field of our Negro Missions. When he visits the various sections of the field, he improves the opportunity there offered him of carrying to his fellow-workers the cheer and the hope that fills his spirit. On these visits, as well as by his correspondence, he has endeared himself to the laborers in the field and helped them in the solution of their difficult problems and in the expansion of their work.

By skilful and persuasive addresses and lectures, by bright and ingenious pamphlets and tracts, by his interesting articles in the "Missionstaube," by his unceasing correspondence, by the exhaustless and contagious enthusiasm displayed by him whenever he advocates the cause, he has helped to lift the Negro Mission enterprise to a new and larger place in the thought, in the giving, and in the devotion of the Synodical Conference.

As the writer of this foreword read the pages of this book, it seemed to him that they reflected the qualities of character and spirit which have endeared Director Drewes to us: his loyalty to truth, his thoughtfulness, his candor and sincerity. And it is the conviction of the undersigned that others who know the Director will also recall these qualities and other traits, which make us, who know him best, trust and love him, as they read this record of a half-century of divine blessings.

F. J. LANKENAU.

I. God Meant It unto Good.

"About the last of August [1619] came in a Dutch man-of-Warre, and sold us twenty negars." With these words Master John Rolfe records the landing of the first African slaves on the North American continent, at Jamestown, Virginia. Two hundred and forty-three years later a slaver landed the last human cargo of slaves from Africa, at Mobile, Alabama. In the year 1860 the total number of slaves in our country was 3,953,760.

A BLESSING IN DISGUISE.

We all thank God that human slavery is a thing of the past in the United States. Yet it remains true that God in His wisdom brought good out of this evil. Joseph was sold into slavery by his own brothers. Forty years later he said to his brothers in Egypt: "Ye thought evil against me, but God meant it unto good, to bring to pass, as it is this day, to save much people alive." Even so God brought good out of the evil of slavery. Said Sandy Alston, of Mount Pleasant, N. C., to the writer: "My mother's father was ten years old when he was brought over from Africa. The good Lord brought them here so that they might get a little knowledge." He meant the knowledge of salvation. In their savage state over in Africa they were blind heathen. They knew nothing of the true God, who made heaven and earth and sent His only-begotten Son into the world to save the world. Their religion was animistic. Animism is the belief "that the spirits of the dead can return and wreak vengeance on their enemies or cause the death of those they wish to have with them." This belief makes the animist a slave of fear. In this fear he goes to the medicine-man. "The medicine-man is the powerful personage with the spirits. To him the people go when ill or unlucky. Sickness is not ascribed to natural causes, but is proof that the sufferer has been bewitched — by an enemy, of course."

From this pagan religion of fear the Africans who were brought to this country as slaves would never have been set free if they had remained in the Dark Continent. They would never have been brought out of darkness into the marvelous light of the true God. So God manifested His mercy in bringing them over. This truth is beautifully expressed by Phyllis

Wheatley, who was brought to America in 1761, when but a child of eight, and was bought by John Wheatley, of Boston: —

'Twas mercy brought me from my pagan land,
Taught my benighted soul to understand
That there's a God — that there's a Savior too;
Once I redemption neither sought nor knew.

Many of the slaveholders were Christians and took an interest in the spiritual welfare of their slaves. They took them along to their churches. In many churches the long galleries were set apart for their use, or there were screened pews for them. In some instances separate churches were built for them, where white pastors or approved colored ministers preached to them.

The first organized effort to give religious instruction to the colored people in the American colonies was made in 1702 in South Carolina by missionaries of the London Society for the Propagation of the Gospel. The Moravians began their work among the Negroes in South Carolina in 1738. The Presbyterians began their work of evangelizing the slaves in 1747, at Hanover, Va. Nineteen years later the Methodists followed and in 1773 the Baptists. In 1859 the Baptists had 175,000, and the Methodists 215,000, baptized members enrolled.

WHAT LUTHERANS DID FOR THE SLAVES.

The Lutheran Church was not numerically strong in the Slave States. The Lutheran Salzburgers, who settled in Georgia as early as 1734, were opposed to human slavery. In 1860 the Synod of Georgia had 312 confirmed members, of whom 54 were colored. The Synod of South Carolina, which was organized in 1824, had 70 colored confirmed members in 1840, while its white membership was 1,622. In 1862 the South Carolina Synod had 4,120 white and 954 colored confirmed members. In 1868 the figures were 3,289 and 144. The Rev. Dr. John Bachman, pastor of St. John's Church, Charleston, S. C., for fifty-six years, was particularly interested in the spiritual welfare of the colored man. He confirmed a boy by the name of Daniel Payne, instructed him privately, and then sent him to the Lutheran Seminary at Gettysburg, Pa., to study for the ministry. Payne graduated in 1823, at the age of twenty-two. Unfortunately, they could find no field for him in the Lutheran Church and advised him to go to the Methodists. What a sad commentary on the Lutheranism of those days! Payne joined the African Methodist Episcopal Church, which had been organized at Philadelphia in 1816, and became one of its greatest bishops. "In many respects Bishop Payne was one of the most remarkable Negro preachers that this country has ever produced."

The North Carolina Synod, organized in 1803, also had a good many churches with regularly confirmed members who were the slaves of white members. Some of these churches even provided a place for the burial of these members. At Old Organ Church in Rowan County, N. C., the marks of the old colored Lutheran graveyard are still to be seen.

Some of the pastors of the old Tennessee Synod, organized in 1820, looked after the spiritual interests of the slaves belonging to the members of their churches. They baptized the children of the slaves, instructed and confirmed them, and administered the Lord's Supper to them. This was particularly true of the pastors of St. John's Church, near Conover, N. C. St. John's did not dismiss and desert its colored members after the Civil War, as was done by so many other Lutheran congregations in the South. Sophronia Hull, her sister Julia Mobley, and three other colored communicant members were still in connection with good old St. John's in 1895.

SOPHRONIA HULL.

This Lutheran ex-slave was born January 22, 1845, near Conover. She was baptized by Rev. Adam Smith of St. John's Church. At the age of fifteen she was confirmed by the distinguished Pastor Polycarp Henkel. By the grace of God she kept the solemn promise made at her confirmation. Her grandfather, Thomas Frye, also called Thomas Smyer, was born on George Washington's plantation at Mount Vernon, Va. Thence he was brought to North Carolina. While tending the still of his master near Catawba, he studied the Lutheran Confessions. In 1868 he was licensed to preach by the Tennessee Synod. He was, therefore, perhaps the first colored Lutheran minister licensed to preach in the Carolinas. However, owing to his advanced age he was not privileged to preach longer than about three months. In the fall of 1923 the writer visited Sophronia Hull in her home. The house was neat and clean. Soon I noticed a book on the table which one does not see very often even in white Lutheran homes. It was a copy of the Book of Concord, which contains all the confessional writings of the Lutheran Church. I was pleasantly surprised and asked, "Do you read in this book?" Her modest answer was, "Yes, sir; I read in it right smart." Paging the book, I noticed that she had told the truth. She departed this life at the ripe old age of 80 years, 2 months, and 11 days. Her pastor says: "Sister Hull was a staunch Lutheran all her life. She loved her Church and its doctrines. Even in her old

Sophronia Hull, Catawba, N. C.

age she never missed a service, and she taught her Sunday-school class every Sunday. She was conscious till death and fell asleep in Jesus, praying to the Great Physician of her soul till the end."

A SAD FALLING AWAY.

When slavery was abolished in our country, many Negroes left the church of their former masters. This was true also in the case of many colored Lutherans. They fell a prey to noisy revivalists. But, thank God, not all fell away from the Church of the Reformation. There were cases of beautiful loyalty. As late as 1870 the Georgia Synod reported colored communicants and accessions from among colored people. Four years before that, in 1866, Dr. D. M. Gilbert said in his address to the Georgia Synod: —

"Suddenly and without any preparation, thrown upon their own resources as they have been, the freedmen stand more in need now than ever in the past of our sympathy and aid. Notwithstanding the bad conduct of some, who through ignorance have suffered themselves to be prejudiced against those who have always been their best friends, let us do what we can to have them all treated with kindness and forbearance and to encourage and forward all proper schemes for their advancement and well-being for this world and for the world to come."

CAUSES OF THE DEFECTION.

You ask, "Why were the former Lutheran slaves allowed gradually to drift away from the Church? Why did the white Lutherans in the South fail to do energetic mission-work among their colored neighbors?" A Southern Lutheran writer answers: "One reason was the disorganized condition of the Southern Lutheran Church after the [Civil] War. Another was the paucity of her ministers and the poverty of her members. A third was the urgent need of looking after, and caring for, her white members, who were relatively in the majority and were widely dispersed. These groups of scattered sheep demanded her pastoral care, and there were wanting the men and the means to raise up suddenly a colored ministry for the colored people."

Another writer says: "The poverty of the white people made it scarcely possible at this time to support churches for themselves, and all missionary work was necessarily suspended; and this was at the very time when the Negro's temptation was greatest to break away from all religious restraints and indulge in sinful excesses."

COLORED LUTHERAN PASTORS.

In spite of their poverty the Lutheran churches of the South did a little for the religious education and training of their former slaves. We have heard of Thomas Frye, whom the Tennessee Synod, in 1868, licensed to preach. In the same year the North Carolina Synod licensed Michael Coble, of Alamance County, N. C. A year later his official report to the synod showed two congregations and two Sunday-schools.

In 1876 we hear of three colored ministers, David Koonts, Samuel Holt, and Michael Coble, who were examined by Rev. C. H. Bernheim and Rev. E. P. Parker. As they passed a satisfactory examination, their license to preach was renewed.

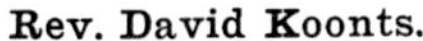

Rev. David Koonts.

Rev. Samuel Holt.

They were induced to organize a conference. These three pastors had attended no school of higher learning and no theological seminary. Their knowledge of true Lutheranism was limited. During a revival Coble went over to the Methodists.

II. Northern Lutherans Enter the Field of Colored Missions.

In 1869 Dr. Walther, the great leader of the Lutheran Synod of Missouri, Ohio, and Other States and one of the greatest theologians of his time, wrote a letter to Rev. F. Sievers, in which he said, among other things: "It will be difficult to begin mission-work among the colored people so long as we have not more men who are conversant with the English language."

Der Lutheraner, the official German organ of the Missouri Synod, said in 1876: "That the poor Negroes of the South are totally sinking into spiritual decay and relapsing into paganism may be understood when one considers the class of ignorant and immoral preachers they have. Will the Lutheran Church, then, not also do something that these political freedmen may become freedmen in the Lord? Should not this mission lie closer to our hearts than missions in foreign countries?"

THE SYNODICAL CONFERENCE RESOLVES TO BEGIN MISSION-WORK AMONG THE FREEDMEN.

July 10, 1872, six Lutheran synods in the United States organized the Evangelical Lutheran Synodical Conference of North America. "The Synodical Conference accepts the canonical Scriptures of the Old and the New Testament as the Word of God and also the symbolical books of the Evangelical Lutheran Church, constituting the Book of Concord of 1580." The following Lutheran synods belong to the Synodical Conference: The Synod of Missouri, Ohio, and Other States; the Joint Synod of Wisconsin and Other States; the Slovak Evangelical Lutheran Synod of America; the Norwegian Evangelical Lutheran Synod. These four synods have over 4,325 congregations and 1,285,000 baptized members. The congregations are chiefly in the North and West.

July 18 to 24, 1877, the Synodical Conference held its convention in Emmanuel Church, Fort Wayne, Ind. This meeting marks the beginning of our Colored Missions. A committee drew attention to an overture submitted by the retiring President, Rev. H. A. Preus, of the Norwegian Synod. In this overture he asked "whether the time had not come for the Synodical Conference to direct its attention to mission-work among the heathen and to start a mission, perhaps, among the Negroes and Indians of this country."

This matter was in full agreement with the constitution of the Synodical Conference. The paragraph on "scope of activities" mentions "matters pertaining to home and foreign mission-work, as also to mission-work among immigrants." So the overture was received with enthusiasm. The delegates were all heartily in favor of launching a mission-project. The only question was: "How shall we start this work? Among which people shall we begin?" Here it was Rev. J. F. Buenger, pastor of Immanuel Lutheran Church in St. Louis, who championed the cause of Colored Missions. He, G. F. H. Meiser, and J. G. Thieme were made members of a committee which was to work out and submit plans for beginning a mission. The committee recommended that a mission be begun and carried on among the religiously neglected and forsaken Negroes of this country. The recommendation was unanimously adopted.

THE MISSION BOARD.

The convention immediately proceeded to elect a mission board and to put the management of its Colored Missions into its hands. The following three members were elected: Rev. John Frederick Buenger, pastor of Immanuel Church, St. Louis; Rev. C. F. W. Sapper, pastor of St. Trinity Church in South

Rev. J. F. Buenger,
First Chairman.

Rev. C. F. W. Sapper,
First Secretary.

St. Louis (he served twenty-one years); Mr. John Umbach, a member of Pastor Buenger's congregation. Buenger was chosen chairman; Sapper, secretary; and Umbach, treasurer.

During the past fifty years the Mission Board has had many prominent Lutherans as members; for example, the following five professors of Concordia Theological Seminary in St. Louis: Prof. F. Pieper, D. D.; Prof. L. Fuerbringer, D. D.; Prof. George Mezger, D. D.; Prof. Theodore Graebner, editor of the *Lutheran Witness;* Prof. Otto C. A. Boecler. Besides these the following may be mentioned: Rev. Charles F. Obermeyer, who served eighteen years; Rev. J. J. Bernthal, president of the Western District of the Missouri Synod; Rev. Richard Kretzschmar, the present president of the same District; Rev. Herman Meyer, president of the Minnesota District; and others.

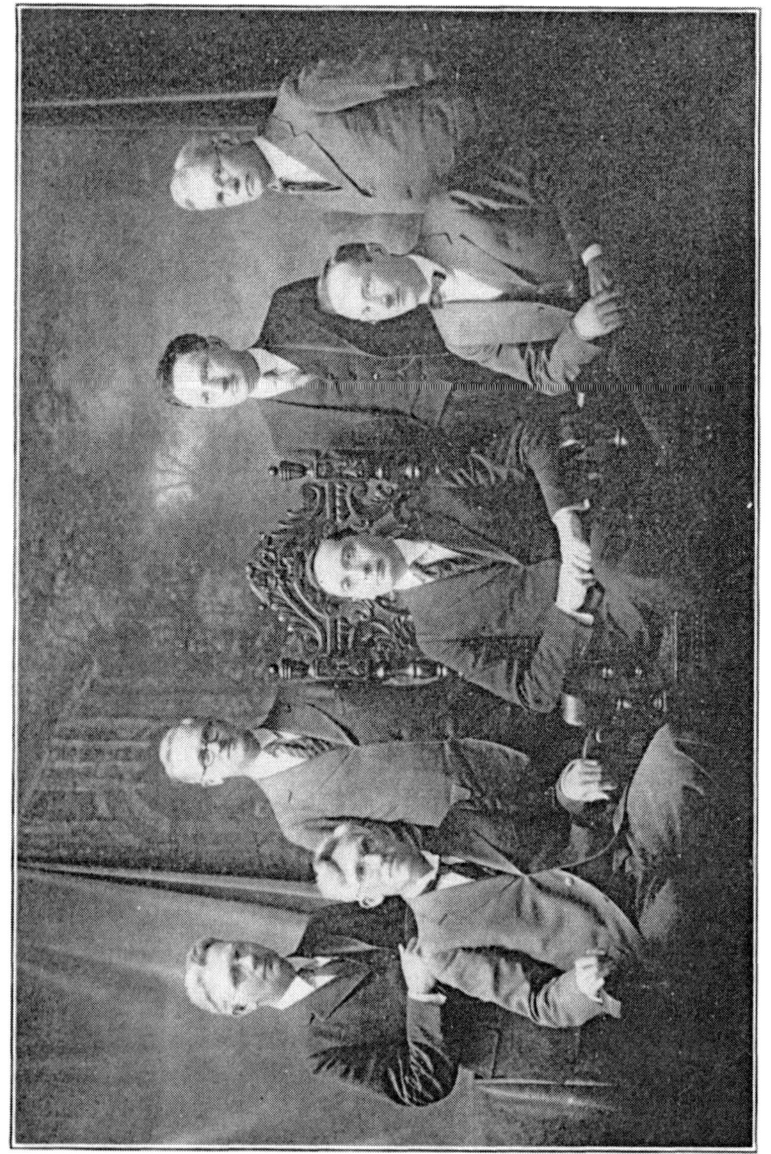

Our Mission Board in 1926.

Front row, left to right: Dir. C. F. Drewes, Prof. Theo. Graebner, Mr. Theo. Eckhart.
Second row: President Im. Albrecht, Rev. Theo. Walther, Rev. L. A. Wisler, Rev. W. Hoenecke.

At the present time the Mission Board is composed of these members: Prof. Theodore Graebner, chairman of the Board, a member since January 20, 1921; Rev. Christopher F. Drewes, Director of Missions, a member since August, 1908; Mr. Theodore W. Eckhart, treasurer, since August, 1924; Rev. Louis A. Wisler, secretary, since September, 1908; Rev. Theodore F. Walther, a grandson of Dr. C. F. W. Walther, a member since September 14, 1916; Rev. Immanuel F. Albrecht, president of the Minnesota District of the Wisconsin Synod, since 1921; Rev. Walter A. Hoenecke, a son of the great dogmatician of the Wisconsin Synod and editor of the *Gemeindeblatt,* the official German organ of the Wisconsin Synod, since 1921; Rev. Jacob Thoen, of the Norwegian Synod, since August, 1926; Rev. John Daniel, of the Slovak Synod, since August, 1926.

Prof. O. C. A. Boecler.
Member of Board
since August, 1926.

Meetings of the full Board are held twice a year in St. Louis; in addition, the members residing in St. Louis meet four times a year. During the time between sessions the Executive Committee, which consists of the chairman, the treasurer, and the Director of Missions, looks after the affairs of the Missions.

III. Our First Missionary Explores the Southland.

As soon as the first Board had been chosen, it took steps to inaugurate the good work. *Rev. John Frederick Doescher* was recommended to the Board as a tried and experienced missionary. He was at that time traveling missionary of the Missouri Synod, residing at Yankton, Dakota Territory. Doescher had entered the ministry at the age of twenty and was now thirty-seven years, married, and the father of a large family. During the first fifteen years of his ministry he had labored in Iowa. The writer did not know Doescher personally, but he has been told that he was an enthusiastic worker, a man of great personal magnetism, warm heart, and sympathetic nature; that his appearance was quite ordinary, but that in the pulpit he soon warmed up and preached eloquently.

A teacher in New Orleans who knew Doescher says: "He was a powerful speaker and drew crowds; but he could not hold people." Having acquired a good working knowledge of English and suffering from the extreme Northern winters, he accepted the call extended to him by the Mission Board. He took his family to Fort Wayne and then repaired to St. Louis to meet the Mission Board and to receive instructions. He was instructed to travel through the Southern States, to preach to

Rev. J. Thoen, Norwegian Synod.
Member of Board.

Rev. J. Daniel, Slovak Synod.
Member of Board.

Negroes where opportunity offered itself, to observe the spiritual condition of the people, and to mark those places which seemed most promising as prospective mission-centers.

DOESCHER'S ORDINATION AS MISSIONARY.

The Western District of the Missouri Synod soon met at Altenburg, Perry Co., Mo. There our pioneer missionary was solemnly commissioned for his work in a beautiful service held Sunday night, October 16, 1877. Rev. Buenger, assisted by Rev. Sapper, performed the ceremony in the presence of a large congregation.

Several days later Rev. Doescher began his missionary activity at New Wells, a Lutheran settlement several miles south of Altenburg. He had been invited to preach an English sermon at the mission-festival in Immanuel Church. Some colored people had been invited to the meeting, and they came. Doescher promised to return.

DOESCHER STARTS ON HIS TOUR OF EXPLORATION.

At Wittenberg Landing our missionary boarded a Mississippi steamboat for Memphis. In Memphis Rev. Henry Sieck, pastor of Trinity Church, was his host. Having preached to colored people six times in four different parts of the city, Doescher left for Little Rock, Ark., where he arrived November 7. In Little Rock he found willing helpers in Rev. C. F. Obermeyer, pastor of the white Lutheran church, and his teacher, C. D. Markworth. At that time Little Rock had a colored population of 6,000, two-fifths of whom were pagan or churchless. The missionary visited the homes of a number of colored people and had religious talks with them. The following Sunday two services were held in Fletcher's Hall, in the heart of the city. The place had no good reputation, and the attendance at both services was disappointing, although the services had been announced in the paper and by means of 500 placards. A member of the white church paid for this advertising. The following Wednesday Doescher preached in a colored church, where he had about 40 hearers. On the second Sunday the services in Fletcher's Hall were better attended too. Doescher also stopped colored children on the street and talked with them. They attended the public school and Sunday-school, but knew nothing of the Savior who died for them. Having been asked by many parents whether he would also teach the children, he became convinced more and more that our Colored Missions would have to establish schools in order to find favor with the people. Rev. Obermeyer and some of his members confirmed him in this belief. So he resolved to make a beginning by opening a Sunday-school in Little Rock. He found time for this because he had been advised not to go farther South for the present, but to stay in Little Rock till January. Sunday, December 2, the Sunday-school was opened. Two children were present. After a month

Rev. C. F. Obermeyer.

the enrolment had climbed to more than forty. The attendance at services also increased. Teacher Markworth decorated the first Christmas-tree in our Missions. He, Pastor Obermeyer, and several members of the white congregation formed an advisory mission committee. This committee as well as Doescher himself desired that he stay longer; the St. Louis Board, however, insisted that Doescher start on his tour of observation again early in January; it requested Pastor Obermeyer to continue the work at Little Rock with the help of some of his members.

DOESCHER CONTINUES HIS TRAVELS.

January 7, 1878, the missionary left Little Rock, returned to Memphis, and thence traveled through Mississippi, Louisiana, Alabama, Florida, Georgia, and Tennessee, preaching in many cities and on many large plantations. Reaching New Orleans March 8, he was welcomed by members of the Lutheran mission society. After prospecting several days, he located a station at the corner of S. Peters and Erato Sts., in the old "Sailors' Home," near the levee. Here a Sunday-school was opened April 7 with 36 pupils. Teacher Huettmann, Mr. F. J. Odendahl, and other laymen helped in the Sunday-school. The enrolment continued to grow, although Doescher had to leave New Orleans April 16. By the middle of May the enrolment was 156, of whom 35 were adults.

We cannot well give a full account of Doescher's journey. Only a few brief remarks can be made. He reached Moss Point, Miss., April 16, Mobile, Ala., April 29. Pensacola and Milton, Fla., were also visited. May 20 he was in Montgomery, Ala. Thence he went to Eufaula, Ala. June 9 he was in Chattahoochee, Fla. He also visited Quincy, Fla. June 14 he arrived in the state capital, Tallahassee. Then he went to Monticello, from there to Waukeenah, where he was obliged to spend a night with colored people because he could secure no lodging with whites. June 25 he preached in Thomasville, Ga., June 27 in Atlanta, June 28 in Chattanooga, Tenn. July 2 he came to Nashville, and July 4 he was in Altenburg, Mo., again.

Not only in Little Rock and New Orleans, but also at all the other places which he visited, the missionary prospector found promising fields. His sympathetic heart was moved with pity as he saw the poor people groping in the darkness of ignorance, superstition, and sin. Going from place to place, he had preached twice and oftener during a single day. It was a most strenuous task. He had traveled between three and four thousand miles.

At Altenburg he preached the following Sunday in the

Rev. J. F. Doescher,
Our First Missionary.

Lutheran church to the colored people of those parts. From Altenburg he traveled via St. Louis to Fort Wayne to see his family and to report to the Synodical Conference, which met at Fort Wayne July 18 to 24. His report created great interest. However, before the convention was over, he was taken seriously ill. After his recovery he needed a long rest.

DOESCHER IN BALTIMORE.

His need of rest and also the yellow fever which was raging in New Orleans did not permit Rev. Doescher to return to New Orleans, where he was to make his permanent residence. Answering an urgent request of our Lutheran pastors in Baltimore, the Mission Board instructed Doescher to visit that city in the interest of Colored Missions. He preached several times and opened a Sunday-school. A certain Joseph Lewis and Rev. Willis R. Polk, who had been educated for the ministry in the Presbyterian Church at a college in Georgia, were gained by Doescher in Baltimore. Later, Polk was sent to New Orleans and Lewis to Little Rock, where we shall meet them again.

IV. Our First Resident Missionary in Little Rock.

As a resident missionary was needed for the station which had been established in Little Rock, the Board applied to the faculties of the seminaries in St. Louis and Springfield for a theological candidate. The faculty in Springfield suggested Candidate Louis Zahn; but he declined. The St. Louis faculty suggested Candidate Frederick Berg, offering to give him his diploma several months before the graduation of his class. Having passed his examination in a most satisfactory way, Candidate Berg started for Little Rock. He was just a little over twenty-two years of age. He entered upon the discharge of his duties as missionary May 3, 1878. Rev. Obermeyer, Teacher Markworth and wife, Mr. C. F. Penzel, and Mr. and Mrs. Jungkuntz nobly assisted the young missionary.

BERG'S FIRST BAPTISM AND FUNERAL.

June 15, 1878, Rev. Berg was privileged to baptize a sick man half an hour before his death. He had instructed this man and at his urgent request baptized him upon his confession of faith in Christ Jesus. The following day he buried him with Christian honors. This was the first baptism and the first funeral in our Colored Missions.

OUR FIRST CONGREGATION IS ORGANIZED.

Two months after his arrival in Little Rock, on July 3, 1878, Berg organized St. Paul's Colored Lutheran Church with three male members. Joseph Lewis, of Baltimore, was one of them. The newly organized congregation formally chose and called Rev. Berg as its pastor, whereupon Rev. Obermeyer installed him.

OUR FIRST CHAPEL IS DEDICATED.

August 18, 1878, was a day of joy and rejoicing for the missionary and his little flock. On that day a chapel, 25×50 feet, was dedicated to the service of the Triune God. It was the first house of worship built for the colored people by our Synodical Conference. Revs. P. Germann, of Fort Smith, Ark., F. Berg, and C. F. Obermeyer delivered the sermons. Berg's discourse in the afternoon was a baptismal address. He baptized 23 persons: infants, older children, young men and young women, men, women, and even persons white with age.

Rev. Frederick Berg,
Our First Resident Missionary. 1926.

OUR FIRST SCHOOL IS ESTABLISHED.

September 16, 1878, Rev. Berg opened the first Christian day-school in our Missions with 46 pupils. In November the enrolment reached 93. Berg needed help. Student Fr. Koenig of the St. Louis Seminary, later a professor at the Teachers' Seminary in Addison, assisted Berg three months. He was succeeded by Student Henry Frincke, now pastor at Monroe, Mich.

OUR FIRST TEACHER.

At the opening of the school in the fall of 1879, Teacher Ernest Jeske, a graduate of the Lutheran Teachers' Seminary at Addison, Ill., was placed in charge of the intermediate department. Mrs. C. Reed, a member of the church, taught the primary department, while Rev. Berg had charge of the grammar department, or academy. "The last-named, being formed of the most advanced pupils of the school, was designed to furnish — at some future time — the teachers and preachers of our mission-work in the South." Mrs. Reed resigned May 20, 1880. September 1 she was succeeded by a young graduate of the Addison Seminary, Mr. Charles Berg. At the beginning of January, 1881, Teacher Berg was transferred to New Orleans to open a school in St. Paul's.

REV. BERG ACCEPTS A CALL.

One year after the congregation at Little Rock had been organized it numbered 19 communicant members. Berg had baptized 12 adults and 32 children. He had lost 9 confirmed members by apostasy. Being tied down in school and unable to make many missionary visits, the young missionary did not see the success which he desired to see. He also suffered from overwork. When he received a call, in October, 1881, from St. Peter's Church in Adams Co., Ind., he accepted it with the consent of the Board. Thirty years later he reentered the service of our Colored Missions as professor and president of Immanuel Lutheran College in Greensboro, N. C. Four months after Berg had left Little Rock, Teacher Jeske accepted a call to Jackson, Mich. Mr. Jeske is now engaged in business in Wisconsin. The vacancies in church and school were the first of many others that followed. Rev. Obermeyer kindly consented to serve the orphaned congregation as much as time would permit.

OTHER PASTORS OF ST. PAUL'S.

Rev. Ernest Meilaender served from June, 1882, to the day of his death, July 19, 1884. Rev. George Allenbach served from November 10, 1884, to August 24, 1890; Rev. Chas. H. Ruesskamp from September 25, 1892, to October, 1895; Rev. Paul Beinke from October 1, 1915, till July, 1918. During the numerous and long vacancies the pastors of the white Lutheran church in Little Rock kindly looked after the deserted little flock as best they could: Revs. Obermeyer, J. W. Miller, Andrew Baepler, W. J. Kaiser, and, particularly, Adolph H. Poppe, who has nobly come to the rescue twice and has ministered to the loyal remnant, in all, nineteen years. When one considers that Pastor Poppe is serving a congregation numbering 850 souls, one cannot but admire the splendid spirit displayed by him in carrying this extra load all these years. May the Lord abundantly reward his service of love!

A SAMPLE OF LOYALTY.

When Rev. Ruesskamp had left Little Rock, the Board resolved to abandon the mission and to sell the mission-property. This was done. Did the congregation pass out of existence now? Some members, indeed, strayed away and joined other churches, but there was a remnant which continued to adhere to the Lutheran Church. This little flock has been without a minister of its own for more than thirty-eight years. What a splendid example of Lutheran loyalty! The flock to-day consists of twenty-three baptized members. Rev. Poppe conducts services with these every other Sunday in the home of Mrs. Emily Bosley, who joined in 1889.

Ellen Bransford joined the Little Rock congregation June 6, 1880, when she was baptized by Pastor Berg. She remained true to her Lutheran Church to the end, which came November 21, 1914. When her last will and testament was opened, it showed that she had left all her earthly possessions to her dearly beloved Lutheran Church. The legacy amounted to $11,096. Several months later Leah Jones, one of the charter members, passed away in peace. She, too, willed her all to the Church, one half going to the white Lutheran church in Little Rock, the other half — $946.80 — to the Colored Missions. The example of the Little Rock mission clearly shows that God is able to make good, loyal Lutherans of colored people, who remain faithful despite adverse and discouraging circumstances.

V. Doescher's Work in New Orleans.

In December, 1878, we see our pioneer missionary preparing to move with his family from Fort Wayne to New Orleans to make that city, with its large colored population, his home.

Doescher found the Sunday-school which he had established April 7 in "Sailors' Home" in a flourishing condition. Teacher Huettmann, who was assisted by two young men (B. Pohlmann and K. Keller) and two young ladies (Miss E. Wendt and Miss E. Smul), all members of Zion Congregation, worked in the Sunday-school with untiring zeal. The old building, in which stood the cradle of our Colored Missions in New Orleans, calls for a description. It reminds us of the miserable shacks in which our good missionaries were obliged to work very often from the beginning to the present time. So let us look at

"SAILORS' HOME."

This once handsome four-story brick structure, destroyed by fire about the year 1897, had served as a boarding-house, hospital, and refuge for indigent sailors, as well as a rendezvous for sailors generally from all parts of the globe. After Rev. Sapper had visited the building in April, 1881, he gave this pen picture of "Sailors' Home": —

"The whole structure is a dark, spooky-looking ruin. The doors and windows are demolished; even some of the door and window frames have been torn out, and along with them went parts of the wall. Here and there the walls have fallen into the rooms, crashing through the floor and ceiling of the rooms below. The whole is a labyrinth of half-demolished rooms, halls, and stairways, filled with filth and refuse, which afford hiding-places for all kinds of vermin, homeless cats and dogs, and the lowest riffraff, who wish to commit sin and shame, for the latter in particular, for the whole neighborhood is fearfully degraded.

"In one of the wings of this horrible building our mission has its home. Not without a secret shudder did I enter, climbing up the staircase, which has been slightly repaired with rough boards (the original staircase has disappeared long ago), and going up to the second story, where a large hall, which is in a somewhat better state of preservation and is divided into two parts by means of a partition, has been put in order for our mission; but even here one may use an umbrella to good advantage when it is raining."

When asked why he selected so degraded a section of the city while other localities contained a much better class of colored people, Doescher replied: "I feel convinced that this neighborhood will furnish the poor and the maimed and the halt and the blind for God's feast." Pews were furnished by Zion Congregation. With these and a borrowed organ the church outfit was complete. The missionary called his place of worship "Mount Zion Evangelical Lutheran Mission Hall." In 1880 we hear him express a desire for a better place of worship.

DOESCHER OPENS A DAY-SCHOOL.

January 6, 1879, the missionary opened a Christian day-school in "Sailor's Home" with 26 pupils. By the end of the month the enrolment had reached 120. He taught school himself. At first his daughter Mary assisted him as much as possible. The strain of trying to keep all those children who were unaccustomed to discipline in order and to teach them was too much for him, and he began to complain that his old heart trouble was returning. So the Board finally permitted him to call Rev. Willis R. Polk from Baltimore to be his assistant. He arrived in March. As Polk was not able to handle that crowd of children alone, a Sunday-school teacher by the name of Louise Watson was engaged. She had been educated and trained for the teaching profession and had been teaching in a public school several terms. Polk was a poor teacher, but a good man in the pulpit; so he assisted in preaching and in teaching the Sunday-school, which Doescher opened in the "Greens" in March. He resigned April 16, 1880, because he felt himself slighted by

Doescher and the Board. Now Louise Watson was alone in the school. She served till December, 1882, when she resigned and went over to the Baptists. She, too, felt herself slighted.

THE FIRST CONFIRMATION IN MOUNT ZION.

After previous instruction seven persons were confirmed by Doescher on Sunday, April 20, 1879: Willis R. Polk, Henry Ford and his wife Emma, Nancy Butler, Eudocia Carter, Sarah Lewis, and Martha Johnson. Some time after this seven other adults were received into the Church by confirmation: Mary Jones, Indiana Buchanon, Rebekka Johnson, Alodie Conklin, Cecilia Seymore, Hezekiah Ford, and Louise Watson.

THE BEGINNING OF ST. PAUL'S CHURCH.

Doescher deemed it necessary to begin work in another part of the city, in the Third District, the so-called "Greens." There he had found many churchless people, most of them Creoles. Early in 1879 a modest building of undressed lumber was put up on a rented site on N. Claiborne St., near Annette. The cost was $300. Doescher begged this money from the committee which had charge of the unused surplus of money given the previous year for the sick and needy during the yellow fever epidemic. The building, 20×30 feet, was dedicated March 9, 1879. The enemies called it the "Chicken-coop." It now stands in the rear of St. Paul's School and is occupied by the janitor. In the new chapel a Sunday-school was opened at once with 17 pupils. Teacher Charles W. Sauer, of St. Paul's white Lutheran church, was put in charge of the Sunday-school. Teachers J. H. Schoenhardt and Koehnke assisted. Preaching services were held every Sunday and every Tuesday night. Polk did most of the preaching. The attendance was poor before long. The Sunday-school, too, showed but little success. But it is not correct to say that the station was ever closed. The records show that there were 25 pupils present in Sunday-school in April, 1880. During the summer of this year, Teacher Sauer attended a meeting of the Mission Board in St. Louis and informed the Board that the advisory committee of fourteen in New Orleans advised to move the chapel to the neighborhood of "Sailors' Home" or to sell it. However, this plan seemed premature to the members of the Board. They resolved that an attempt should be made to get the mission going by means of a school. Accordingly, Teacher Charles Berg was transferred from Little Rock to New Orleans. He opened St. Paul's School January 26, 1881, with five pupils. The Lord blessed his labors to such an extent that in April he had 90 pupils in his school. We shall hear more of this excellent teacher later.

DOESCHER ACCEPTS A CALL TO A WHITE CONGREGATION.

During the yellow fever epidemic in 1878 Rev. Baumann, pastor of St. John's Church in New Orleans, died in the middle of September; also his wife. The congregation requested the Mission Board to permit Rev. Doescher to serve it during the vacancy in addition to serving his two mission-stations. The request was granted, and the Doescher family moved into the vacant parsonage. March 16, 1879, the congregation extended a call to our missionary. He accepted the call under the express condition that he be permitted to preach to the colored people as heretofore. The condition was accepted by the members of St. John's. The Mission Board, however, clearly saw that this would not do in the long run and took steps to secure another missionary. But all its efforts seemed to be in vain. At last, in the summer of 1880, the professors of the St. Louis Seminary recommended one of its students who was to graduate the end of June. He was a Norwegian, and his name was Nils Jules Bakke.

VI. Doescher is Succeeded by Bakke.

Candidate Bakke, a physically strong and mentally bright young man twenty-eight years of age, accepted the call into the Colored Missions and remained in the service to the end of his life, for more than forty years. November 7, 1880, Bakke was ordained by Rev. Buenger in Immanuel Church, St. Louis. The following Tuesday he and Miss Concordia Guenther, daughter of Prof. Martin Guenther of Concordia Seminary, were joined in holy wedlock. The following Sunday they were in New Orleans. Rev. Doescher installed the new missionary as his successor.

Rev. Bakke preached every Sunday in "Sailors' Home" and beginning with May 29, 1881, also in the little chapel on N. Claiborne St. At first he also had to teach school. Before long the members sent a petition to the Board in St. Louis, asking that their former pastor be given back to them. It was not hard to see who had put them up to this. But still greater trouble was to come. Bakke says: "On account of the controversy concerning the doctrine of election, Rev. Doescher, in 1882, severed his connection with the Synodical Conference and joined the Ohio Synod, and the members he had confirmed, followed him. Some, however, returned. The new missionary labored for two years with small success in 'Sailors' Home.' Only two women were gained." These two women were Margaret Mosely and Mary C. Wright, who were confirmed October 7, 1882. Mary C. Wright had been born on the Island of St. Thomas, confirmed in the Lutheran Church at Greencastle, Pa., in 1846, and had come to New Orleans in 1862. At first she attended services in a white Lutheran church in New Orleans. She remained true to her Church till her death, November 22, 1923. In December 1882, Mount Zion Church and School were able to move into a building at the corner of Thalia and Franklin, about half a mile west of "Sailors' Home." The Board had bought a large old church from the Presbyterians. "From that time on the work of the Lord began to prosper." Bakke served Mount Zion together with St. Paul's till August 10, 1891.

Rev. N. J. Bakke in 1918.

PROGRESS AT ST. PAUL'S.

Teacher Charles Berg and his school were fountains of blessings for the mission-station out in the "Greens." The school grew by leaps and bounds, until the "Chicken-coop" could not contain the crowd any longer. Berg treated his pupils with kindness and love. He was held in love and esteem by nearly every one who knew him. The pupils brought their parents and other relatives to church; and so it was made possible for the missionary to organize a small congregation. Bakke himself paid this tribute to his teacher: "Berg was an excellent teacher and a capable worker, and his labor was signally blessed. The first members and founders of St. Paul's Congregation were children educated in his school. After seven years the Lord summoned His faithful servant to His heavenly mansions. He died March 9, 1888, and was buried in the cemetery of the Evangelical Lutheran St. John's Church." After Berg's death Student F. J. Lankenau took charge of Berg's school till the end of the term.

THE FIRST CONFIRMATION CLASS IN ST. PAUL'S.

When school opened again in the fall of 1881, the missionary organized a class of eight catechumens. After a year these catechumens had so far advanced in Christian knowledge that they might have been confirmed. Pastor and teacher were happy. But their joy was turned into sorrow. All the catechumens stepped back. The missionary felt like leaving. But, lo and behold, after a few days three of the children returned. The Lord had led them to reconsider the matter. They desired to be confirmed and to become members of the Lutheran Church. It is easy to imagine the joy of the missionary. Now the ice was broken. The three applicants were confirmed October 15, 1882. Their names were Josephine Williams, Louis Thomas, and Frank Royal (Francois). Josephine has broken her confirmation vow and had to be excommunicated as a public sinner. Frank Francois died in connection with the Lutheran Church two years ago. Louis Thomas is by the grace of God a member in good standing to this day. May the merciful Savior keep him faithful unto death and give him a crown of life!

Louis Thomas,
St. Paul's, New Orleans.

SECTARIAN OPPOSITION.

Rev. E. H. Wildgrube, pastor of St. Paul's, says in a letter received by the writer: "It may interest you to hear of the opposition which our first missionaries and the newly confirmed had to face. In those days the Baptists and Methodists had a strong hold on the colored people here, and they did all in their power to keep the Lutherans from making headway. The Baptist and the Methodist preacher formed an alliance, had posters printed and posted which informed the colored people that the Lutheran Church was 'the devil's church' and the Lutheran school 'the devil's synagog.' When the first class was ready for confirmation, the news was brought to the relatives of the children, who then tried to scare the children, telling them that they would become the devil's children by confirmation. And when the newly confirmed wanted to go to the Lord's Supper, they were told that they would surely be lost. The poor children knew not what to believe. However, three of the children were moved by the Spirit of God to come through and to confess their Savior before men by confirmation." Louis Thomas did not only overcome the threatening and the coaxing of his parents, but he succeeded in winning them and other relatives for Christ and His true visible Church on earth.

NEW CHURCH AND SCHOOL.

May 1, 1883, the Mission Board bought a lot on Annette St., between N. Claiborne and Derbigny, and during the summer vacation the "Chicken-coop" was moved from the rented place to this new place and repaired. In September of the same year 112 children tried to attend Teacher Berg's school; however, only 92 could be accommodated. Under the circumstances it became necessary to provide larger quarters; but it took several years before funds were available for this purpose. The new chapel was dedicated September 23, 1888; the two-story new school was dedicated March 8, 1891. The school is in disuse since last year. Its occupants moved into Luther College, which adjoins St. Paul's Station. Five months after the dedication of the school Rev. Bakke followed the instructions of the Board and left for the new field in North Carolina. He left New Orleans August 10, 1891, going via St. Louis to Concord, N. C. When he left, Mount Zion had about 240 baptized members, and St. Paul's had about 136.

REV. FRANCIS J. LANKENAU SUCCEEDS REV. BAKKE.

Candidate F. J. Lankenau, from the Seminary in Springfield, Ill., was called as Bakke's successor in New Orleans. On Sunday, August 30, 1891, he preached his introductory sermon. He remained seventeen years, working with zeal, energy, and success. Lankenau was not a stranger in New Orleans, having taught in St. Paul's School after Teacher Berg's death, in March, 1888. The colored people had confidence in him. His former pupils welcomed him with smiling faces. The membership rapidly increased. He also had charge of Mount Zion till May 1, 1894, when Rev. Edward Kuss was transferred from

Carrollton to Mount Zion. However, Kuss left again after three years, accepting a call to Zion Lutheran Church in New Orleans; and now Rev. Lankenau was in charge of Mount Zion again till young Rev. K. Kretzschmar was installed on September 2, 1900. Meanwhile Rev. F. W. Siebelitz was his assistant in church and school from November 14, 1897, to January, 1900. During Rev. Lankenau's incumbency the membership of St. Paul's increased from 136 to 315. More will be said of him in a later section.

OTHER PASTORS OF ST. PAUL'S.

During the long vacancy which followed Rev. Lankenau's departure from New Orleans in September, 1908, St. Paul's was supplied by Prof. Frederick Wenger, who also succeeded him as president of Luther College. Professor Wenger is now professor at Concordia College in Springfield, Ill. Rev. Albert Witt, of Niagara County, N. Y., served St. Paul's for about nine months, from September 26, 1909, to August, 1910. He accepted a call from St. John's Church, the same congregation which had called Doescher. Witt's successor was the Rev. Edward H. Schmidt, who had entered the service of our Colored Missions at Napoleonville, La., May 10, 1908, and had also served as supply pastor at Mansura, La. Rev. Schmidt was installed in St. Paul's October 23, 1910, and served till July, 1918. During the eight and a half years of his pastorate in St. Paul's the congregation continued to grow. Although Trinity was branched off in January, 1912, St. Paul's was still the largest congregation in the entire Mission. The Mission Board and his colleagues in New Orleans were sorry to see him accept the position of chaplain in the Army. He left July 28, 1918, after having served for ten years with success. During the vacancy which followed, Prof. Hugo Meibohm, of Luther College, faithfully served the congregation with the means of grace until Rev. Miles Gebauer arrived August 26, 1919. October 16, 1921, the members, who had learned to love their new pastor, regretfully consented to let him accept a call to Calvary Congregation in New Orleans. The present pastor, Rev. E. H. Wildgrube, was installed March 5, 1922. He also served Trinity until November, 1925, and again since April, 1927. He is serving our largest congregation in all faithfulness.

ST. PAUL'S SCHOOL.

Since the days of Teacher Charles Berg, who died in March, 1888, St. Paul's School has had many teachers: A. Scheffler, Jacob Kaufmann, Carl F. Lemke, Miss L. Trog, C. H. Heintzen, R. A. Wilde, L. Fuhrmann, Miss Lankenau, Miss Jessie R. Hamann, Napoleon Seeberry, Aaron Wiley, William B. Seeberry, John Thompson, Arthur V. Berger, Miss Sylvina Raymond, Miss Emma Dunn, Miss Mercedes Tervalon, Miss Ruth Bonnafon, Miss Edna Walters, Miss Edna Thomas,

Our St. Paul's School in New Orleans, La., 1926.

Left: Teacher Wm. Seeberry and Missionary E. H. Wildgrube. Right: Teachers S. Raymond and A. Berger.

Miss Adeline Winn, and Miss Sophia Raymond. The present teaching force consists of Mr. Wm. B. Seeberry (since September, 1908), Mr. Arthur V. Berger (since 1922), and Miss Sylvina Raymond (since 1913).

At the beginning of 1927 the school had an enrolment of 128. The competition has grown very strong.

Former Teacher Heintzen tells a story of a strict Roman Catholic which shows the good reputation of the school. The man said: "Yes, sir, I's a good Catholic, an' I'se goin' to live an' die a Catholic, too, but I tells you, I likes de Lutheran school. My chillun done learned very well dere. I'se mo' dan satisfied an' tells dat to my frens. Mos' of de people here owes deir edication an' what erubiments dey's got to your school; an' judgin' by deir edication, de school mus' be good."

Here is a story which illustrates the good influence which the school has had on that part of the city, the "Greens." Said an old mammy: "O teacher, it was terrible here before your Church began to work among the poor colored people, to be sure. Dere was nothin' but gamblin' an' dancin', fightin' an' shootin', every day, worst on Sunday. Out in de 'Green' one wasn't safe after dark. But look at de change now! Most of de people livin' in de 'Green' went to your school an' learned to be good, an' many are members of your Church. An' you teach dem to work an' mind deir families an' raise deir chillun right, to be sure. Your Church did much good, an' our parson, de Reverend Dr. Hall, says so too, to be sure."

OUR OTHER CHURCHES IN NEW ORLEANS.

In the fall of 1885 the Mission Board sent a second missionary to New Orleans, Rev. August Burgdorf, now pastor of a large church in Chicago. He began his work in Carrollton, a suburb of New Orleans. The Board bought an old church. Since the tip of its steeple was ornamented with a metal rooster, the people called it the "Rooster Church." In this church Rev. Burgdorf opened a school, which was taught successively by William Joeckel, Louis E. Gilster, and Julius Moser.

Having meanwhile established another station, Bethlehem, Burgdorf was succeeded in Carrollton by Candidate Edward E. Kuss, from the Seminary in St. Louis, in the fall of 1893. The following year Kuss was transferred to Mount Zion to relieve Rev. Lankenau, and the Carrollton station was closed. It remained closed till the summer of 1912, when Rev. G. M. Kramer of Bethlehem reopened it. Rev. C. Peay served the Carrollton station from April, 1915, to July 30, 1917. After Peay's transfer to Alabama, Rev. Kramer took charge of Concordia, Carrollton, again. Peter Robinson is principal of the school.

BETHLEHEM.

This fourth station in New Orleans was opened by Rev. Burgdorf in 1887. He was successful in showing a number of people the sinfulness of membership in a secret society, or lodge. They withdrew their membership and joined the Lutheran Church.

Rev. August Burgdorf.

In 1895, after ten years of zealous, self-sacrificing labor, Rev. Burgdorf was obliged by ill health to leave New Orleans. Rev. J. W. F. Kossmann succeeded him in November, 1895, and remained in charge of Bethlehem for almost eleven years. The present pastor, Rev. Gotthilf M. Kramer, was installed in Bethlehem on Sunday, August 18, 1907. He has now ministered to the members of Bethlehem for about twenty years. The members of Bethlehem are well indoctrinated. Robert Dixon, born August 5, 1846, and confirmed with his wife by Rev. Burgdorf, is one of the good old loyal members. He is ever thankful to the good Lord for having led him into the Church of the pure Word and Sacraments.

TRINITY CHAPEL.

May 12, 1912, Rev. Ed H. Schmidt, pastor of St. Paul's at that time, began mission-work east of the territory of St. Paul's and then organized Trinity Chapel with several members of St. Paul's. A neat chapel-school was erected in 1916. Rev. Wildgrube has charge of Trinity Chapel. There is a school connected with the church.

Rev. G. M. Kramer and His Confirmation Class in Bethlehem, 1926.

MOUNT ZION.

The reader will remember that Mount Zion, begun in old "Sailors' Home," is our oldest congregation in the Crescent City. Since the days of Bakke, Lankenau, and Kuss the following missionaries have served this church: Rev. Karl Kretzschmar, now in Fort Smith, Ark.; Rev. Ed C. Krause, now in Sheboygan, Wis.; Rev. Albert O. Friedrich, deceased; Rev. Theodore Schliepsiek, now in Vinton, Iowa; Rev. Walter H. Beck, now professor at Immanuel Lutheran College in Greensboro, N. C.; and Rev. Oscar W. Luecke, since September 3, 1925. During five vacancies Pastor Kramer of Bethlehem did supply-work in Mount Zion both faithfully and efficiently. Andrew Seraile,

Teacher Eugene R. Vix.

Teacher D. Meibohm.

Ethel Johnson, and Elsie Gilbert are the present teachers of the school. Two former teachers are deserving of special mention, Teachers Vix and Meibohm.

TEACHER EUGENE R. VIX.

When Rev. Polk had resigned in April, 1880, Mount Zion School was in need of a teacher. In the summer of 1881 Eugene R. Vix, a member of St. John's Church, New Orleans, graduated from the Teachers' Seminary at Addison. As his health was poor, he did not accept a call, but decided to remain at home for a while. December 7, 1881, he was temporarily placed in charge of Mount Zion School. The appointment became permanent. He served in this school till his death, July 10, 1918, all in all 36 years and 7 months. Vix was of a genial disposition and was interested in his work and in his pupils. He was small of stature, but every inch a man and a pedagog. The splendid discipline which the writer observed in Teacher Vix's room, his splendid teaching ability, and the results achieved made an unforgetable impression on him. Perhaps no other white teacher has shown the way to heaven and happiness to so many children as did Mr. "Vick." Hundreds of men and women call his memory blessed. Rev. K. Kretzschmar, who worked with this fine Christian teacher in Mount Zion, says: "Pastors came and went, but these faithful laborers, Vix and Meibohm, were permanent fixtures. Many people at last even forgot that this congregation bears the name of Mount Zion, speaking only of 'Mr. Vix's church.' In the end even the pastor of the church was at times called 'Mr. Vix's pastor.' " Most of the children who sat at his feet would probably never have tasted the Bread of Life if they had not attended his school.

TEACHER DIETRICH MEIBOHM.

Teacher Meibohm came to Mount Zion School November 17, 1893, and served until the infirmities of old age obliged him to tender his resignation, with deep regret, in the spring of 1923, after having devoted three decades of his life to the education and training of colored boys and girls. He died in New Orleans on Sunday morning, June 15, 1924, at a ripe old age. Like his colleague Vix, Meibohm was an excellent teacher. Rev. Lankenau, who had the pleasure of working together with both, writes: "The writer feels that never was another pastor favored with two such teachers as he had in Teachers Vix and Meibohm. In every perplexity he knew that he could go to them for counsel and advice, and when disheartening experience brought his youthful courage to a low ebb, these veterans of the Lord were ever ready to cheer him up."

At the request of the writer to let the public know some of his experiences in school, our modest Teacher Meibohm related the following experience through which the Lord permitted him to see that his work in the school was not in vain. Said he: "One day a well-dressed colored lady came into the schoolyard and asked me whether I was Teacher Meibohm. When I had told her that I was the person she was looking for, she said: 'I come from Defiance, and my sister-in-law, Clara B., who in former years attended your school, asked me to come and bring you her greetings. She told me that she never would have learned to know her Savior if she had not attended your school.' "

ST. PAUL'S AT MANSURA, LA.

About 155 miles northwest of New Orleans, in Avoyelles Parish, lies the large Creole village of Mansura. A large Roman Catholic church was for years the only church far and near. Truly medieval conditions obtained. The people, both colored and white, sat in darkness like unto that of the Dark Ages. It is reported that the parish priest once refused to baptize an infant under the following circumstances: A colored couple was blessed with a pair of twins. Being poor, they offered the usual fee in the case of a baptismal ceremony. However, the priest baptized only one of the twins and told the parents to come back with the other infant when they had the fee. — Here is a case that was reported to Rev. K. Kretzschmar while he served the congregation at Mansura: A man who had lost his wife by death insisted on having a comparatively expensive burial ceremony held over her body. Being poor, he had not the means to pay the priest the fee, but would undoubtedly have done so as soon as he had sold his prospective cotton crop. The priest, however, had not the patience to wait so long. He sent the constable, who confiscated the horses of the poor man while he was working his farm and caring for his crop.

A STRANGE STORY.

Henry Thomas, a member of St. Paul's in New Orleans, was a bird-catcher by profession. This brought him to the neighborhood of Mansura for a while. He took with him his Bible and his Catechism. He found no Lutherans at Mansura. Whenever any one asked him to what church he belonged, he said that he had once been a Roman Catholic, but by reading the Bible had become a Lutheran and had joined a colored Lutheran church in New Orleans.

About two months after Thomas had settled at Mansura, P. M. Lehman, Scott Normand, and Pete Batiest were repairing the chimney of Widow Lehman near Mansura. When their work was done, they sat down to rest and talk a while. The conversation drifted to the treatment which the colored people and their children were receiving at the hands of the priest. Referring to the new church in Mansura, one of the three complained: "We have built a heaven in Mansura, but we cannot get in!" Their children were being neglected, they said. If they only had a school for their children and a church! Thomas happened along. He told them of the work the Lutheran Church was doing in New Orleans and suggested to them that they invite his pastor, the Rev. Lankenau. They requested Thomas to write to his pastor and invite him to come and preach to them.

March 10, 1898, Rev. Lankenau and his assistant, Rev. Siebelitz, went to Mansura. A meeting was announced to be held in the home of Scott Normand, about two and a half miles north of Mansura, in a settlement called Cocoville. A large number of colored people came to the meeting and listened attentively to the preaching of the Gospel and to an exposition of the Bible-doctrines of the Lutheran Church. The people were impressed. They wanted to hear more. So it was arranged to have preaching services once a month by Rev. Lankenau and Rev. Siebelitz alternately.

As the people did not lose their interest in the movement, the Mission Board resolved to build a chapel for them. The people gave two acres of land. On Pentecost Sunday, 1899, the chapel was dedicated. Some people came twenty miles to attend the dedication. October 8, 1899, Rev. Lankenau installed the first resident missionary, Rev. Wm. Pretzch. Since then the following pastors have served the congregation: Martin Weinhold, F. W. Wenzel, Chas. D. Peay, Wilfred Tervalon. The present pastor, Rev. Calvin P. Thompson, is a child of this congregation. He has been its pastor since August, 1925. He also teaches school. Revs. K. Kretzschmar and Ed H. Schmidt served as supply pastors.

St. Paul's Congregation at Cocoville, now called Lutherville, dismissed a number of members to its daughter, Augustana in Alexandria, about thirty-two miles northwest of Mansura; still it has 122 baptized members. The people live on their little farms and do not move away to a great extent.

St. Paul's has furnished more students for the work in church and school than any other congregation in our Colored Missions. Prof. Paul D. Lehman, of Alabama Luther College in Selma; Rev. C. P. Thompson; his brother Rev. John Thompson, of Tilden, Alabama; Rev. E. R. Berger, of Alexandria, La., are all children of this church. Three or four boys of the congregation are now in training at our colleges.

ST. PAUL'S, NAPOLEONVILLE.

About eighty miles west of New Orleans, in Assumption Parish, is the city of Napoleonville. It is in the heart of the country described in Longfellow's *Evangeline*. Here Rev. Lankenau, in June, 1905, established a mission. Owing to the lodge evil and also to the closing of the large sugar-cane mill some years ago, the station has remained small. We own a chapel-school and a parsonage in Napoleonville. Plans are maturing to have the missionary take charge also of the work that has been begun by Rev. Kramer in Baton Rouge, in 1926.

AUGUSTANA, ALEXANDRIA.

Alexandria, about 192 miles northwest of New Orleans, is a pretty and progressive city, to which some of our Mansura members moved in search of employment. Since October, 1915, the respective pastors of our Mansura congregation looked after these members, preaching to them occasionally. June 10, 1923, Rev. W. Tervalon made a beginning of real, regular mission-work. August 14, 1924, Rev. Eugene Berger was put in charge of the promising station. In spite of the lack of a suitable place for services and school, the congregation has grown. A building site has been purchased for $1,879, and when this writing appears in print, the chapel-school, which is to cost $5,900, will perhaps have been dedicated.

STATUS OF OUR MISSIONS IN LOUISIANA.

All told, we have in the Louisiana field 8 churches and 1 preaching-place, 6 pastors, 13 teachers (and 3 pastors also teaching school), 824 pupils in the day-school, 757 in the Sunday-school, 1,187 baptized members, or souls, and 679 confirmed members. The contributions during 1926 were $5,714.03. Rev. G. M. Kramer, pastor of Bethlehem and Concordia, is superintendent of the Louisiana field.

VII. A Memorial of Lutheran Loyalty.

Late in the year 1880 a well-educated Lutheran minister, who had been a missionary among the Gallas in Africa for five years, came with his wife and three children to Green Bay in Prince Edward County, Virginia. He was in search of health. His wife had bought two hundred acres of land near Green Bay. The name of this missionary was W. R. Buehler. He belonged to the Protest Party of the New York Ministerium.

Knowing that their new neighbor had formerly been a missionary in Africa, the colored folks at Green Bay requested Buehler to preach to them and to teach their children. The wretched spiritual condition of the people moved him to pity, and he granted their request. Having heard of the mission of the Synodical Conference, Buehler wrote several letters to the Mission Board in St. Louis late in October, 1880, offering his services. The Board sent a committee to Green Bay to colloquize him. The committee recommended his appointment. Mrs. Buehler kindly donated a piece of land to our mission and also the logs for a chapel-school, which cost about $200 and was dedicated January 8, 1881. April 4, Rev. Buehler opened a school in this log house.

As soon as he had begun to work among the colored people, the white neighbors broke off all neighborly intercourse with him and the members of his family. He and his loved ones were ostracized. Nor was that all. Those whites hatched a plot to beat Buehler so unmercifully that he would be glad to quit. However, having been among savages in Africa, Buehler was not afraid; and the Savior kept His promise: "Lo, I am with you alway, even unto the end of the world."

CHANNIE DOSWELL.

Four miles southwest of Green Bay is Meherrin. The name of the place is from the Tuscarora Indian language and means "An Island in the River." Several miles southeast of Meherrin there is a colored settlement called Doswelltown, so named because of the many Doswells that lived there. Henry Clay Doswell was a carpenter. He reported to his sister-in-law Channie that he had met the Lutheran missionary at Green Bay. She asked Henry Clay to invite Rev. Buehler to come to Meherrin and preach to them. The invitation was accepted, and early in April, 1883, Buehler conducted his first service in the colored school near Meherrin. However, the members of the school board were all members of the Baptist Church, and Buehler was refused permission to use the school. Channie now cheerfully put her cabin in Doswelltown at the disposal of the missionary.

SERVICES UNDER THE WILD CHERRY-TREE.

The services in Channie's home were attended by from twenty to thirty persons. The house was crowded; so when the weather got warm, they had preaching under the large wild cherry-tree in the front yard. Eight of the people expressed their willingness to join the Lutheran Church, and Buehler began to instruct them twice a week. A member of this class says: "Many thought we were foolish. We would learn our hymns and the Catechism line by line just like little children; and how some people would laugh at us! But we did not mind that at all. It was not long before others joined us." The first four persons who joined by confirmation deserve to be mentioned by name: Channie Doswell, Mary A. Doswell, Charles Wall, and his wife Sallie.

THE LOG HOUSE IS MOVED TO DOSWELLTOWN.

When colder weather came, the need of a suitable shelter became pressing. Since the work at Green Bay was a failure, the Buehlers consented to have the log house on their farm

The Famous Cherry-Tree.
Cora Holmes and Mary A. Doswell, seated.

taken down and moved to Doswelltown. The work was done in October, 1883. The people gave the site. The men left their work and helped. Even women and girls lent a helping hand. Channie Doswell hired a white man and his team to do the hauling. Her husband, who had not joined the little flock at the time, complained to her: "Ol' woman, you'll ruin us." She replied: "I don't care if I do. The Lord will take care of us." Mary A. Doswell says: "We whitewashed the log house inside and outside ourselves and now thought we were something. How we did love our minister for the words he spoke!" At Christmas they moved into the church. Two months later Buehler was privileged to baptize twenty-two small and larger children on one day. He taught school, walking the five miles from Green Bay to Meherrin twice a day.

A SEVERE TEST OF LOYALTY.

To the Mission Board it always seemed questionable whether Meherrin was really a mission-field because there were few churchless people there. February 25, 1886, Buehler apprised the Board of the fact that he had received and accepted a call to a high school for girls in Strassburg, Germany. At the same time he requested the Board to send a successor at once. At the end of March he left. Mary Doswell says: "We were sorry at the thought of never seeing him again." During his stop-over in New York City he was called as assistant pastor by Rev. L. Halfmann's congregation. The following year he died in a smallpox hospital in New York.

The Board sent Student S. Hoernicke from Springfield to Meherrin for the time being. He arrived April 2 and informed the people that the Mission Board had sent him to stay only until the Board could ascertain at the meeting of the Synodical Conference, in the month of August, whether its recommendation to abandon Meherrin would be adopted. "Aunt" Channie Doswell, that fervent and zealous worker, said: "We will pray to the Lord that this may never happen. I am sure that He will hear our prayer. He will not forsake us and will not let us fall back into the darkness from which we were rescued." Then she added: "If you quit mission-work here, all these children around us who now are baptized will grow up in darkness, as we once did. We must pray to Him. He will hear our prayer."

What happened at the meeting of the Synodical Conference in August? It was resolved to close the station at Meherrin and to advise the flock of 8 confirmed and 29 baptized members to emigrate to Little Rock, Ark., where they would find a church and school. Little Rock is about a thousand miles from Meherrin. August 25 the Board resolved to recall Student Hoernicke and to ask Rev. Oehlschlaeger, of Richmond, to go to Meherrin and tell the people that they should move to Arkansas. There was much sorrow. They felt forsaken. They could not gather courage to sell and set out for the West.

What did the eight members do when their pastor had left them and the student had been recalled? Did they become churchless, or did they join the sectarian church in their neighborhood? By no means. They met in their log chapel every Sunday; a young man, Henry B. Doswell, was chosen reader, and he read a sermon to them from Luther's House Postil. They also kept up the Sunday-school. Meanwhile they kept on writing to the Board in St. Louis and begging that a pastor be sent to them again. Thus a year passed, and another year came and went. No pastor came.

At the end of two years the Board began to send students from Springfield to supply the station temporarily: D. H. Schoof, Alfred Brauer (now in Australia), and F. J. Lankenau. Thus two more years rolled around, and they were still without a pastor. But the little flock remained loyal and true. Moved by such loyalty to the Lutheran Church, the Synodical Con-

Pastor Dorpat and His Pupils at Meherrin.

ference, in 1890, resolved to resume the work and authorized the Mission Board to call a missionary for Meherrin. Rev. D. H. Schoof was called. When he arrived at Meherrin the middle of September, 1890, the congregation was not only there, but the number of confirmed members had increased from 8 to 34, and the number of baptized members had grown from 29 to 68. What a splendid example of loyalty!

Rev. Schoof was pastor of St. Matthew's at Meherrin seventeen years. During this time thirty-two acres of land were purchased, a chapel-school was built, and a parsonage erected, the first parsonage in our Colored Missions.

During the vacancy which followed after Schoof's departure the congregation was served by Prof. Martin Lochner, Rev. J. S. Koiner, and Student Otho Lynn. Pastor Emil Polzin served as pastor from May 12, 1912, to June 14, 1917; Rev. John W. Fuller was in charge of the congregation from July 1, 1917, to November 21, 1920. The present pastor, Rev. Lawrence G. Dorpat, was installed November 21, 1920. He also teaches school. Although many of the members of St. Matthew's have moved to Yonkers, N. Y., during the past thirty years and joined our church at that place, the congregation still has 156 baptized members and 74 confirmed members, of whom 26 are voting members. The membership is a thoroughly indoctrinated Lutheran body and enjoys the respect of the community. Said a business man of Meherrin to the writer about eleven years ago: "Your missionaries have elevated the morals of the Negroes and are well thought of by the whites."

VIII. A Call from the Old North State.

During the first fourteen years our Colored Missions grew gradually, very gradually. At the end of 1890 there were seven stations: four in New Orleans and one each in Little Rock, Ark., Meherrin, Va., and Springfield, Ill. These were being served by Revs. Bakke, Burgdorf, Allenbach, Schoof, and Knabenschuh. Under their care there were about 630 baptized members. During the following year, 1891, a new and unexpected addition was made to our mission-work. This was in North Carolina.

Attention has been drawn to the fact that there were colored Lutheran pastors and congregations in North Carolina after the Civil War. In 1889 the Synod of North Carolina held its convention in old St. John's Church, in Cabarrus County, about six miles east of the City of Concord. Four colored ministers were present, having voice and vote and being on the same footing with all other members. At this convention the committee on "Work among the Freedmen" recommended "that the colored brethren connected with this Synod be allowed to form themselves into a synod." This recommendation was adopted. The colored ministers and the delegates of their five churches, on their part, petitioned the convention to the like effect. The result was that on Wednesday, May 8, 1889, at 11.30 A. M., in St. John's Church, a colored Lutheran synod was organized, which adopted the name "Alpha Synod of the Evangelical Lutheran Church of Freedmen in America." The new Synod consisted of four pastors and five congregations with about 180 baptized members. Only three of the five congregations had a church of their own. However, the white synod held out prospects of moral and financial support.

THE PASTORS OF THE ALPHA SYNOD.

Rev. David James Koonts had a congregation in Davidson County and in Concord; Rev. Samuel Holt had a small congregation at Springdale, Alamance County; Rev. Nathan Clapp held services twice a month in a public schoolhouse two miles east of Elon College, Alamance County; Rev. Wm. Philo Phifer was holding forth in a lodge-hall in Charlotte. Koonts and Phifer were able to read and write, while Holt and Clapp could read only a little and write not at all. Their theological education and training was very, very meager. Koonts was the ablest man of the quartet and was chosen president of Alpha. As Phifer was the only other man who could write, he was made secretary. A treasurer they had not. There were no funds to be administered. A year and three weeks after Alpha Synod had been organized, its president suddenly died of poisoning. The synod did not die with him. Clapp, Holt, and Phifer held together. Phifer, the ablest one of the three, continued to act as secretary.

THE ALPHA SYNOD APPEALS TO THE SYNODICAL CONFERENCE.

The North Carolina Synod was unable to give much financial support to its young daughter Alpha. In their financial straits the three surviving pastors determined to send an appeal to the Lutherans in the West. They had heard or read of the work of the Synodical Conference, and so Phifer was authorized to write a letter of appeal. He mailed it to Rev. Dr. Henry Schwan, President of the Missouri Synod. The sum and substance of the letter was: Please take steps toward putting the colored Lutheran mission-work in North Carolina in safe hands; we are unable to maintain and extend the work. Dr. Schwan forwarded the letter to the Mission Board in St. Louis. The letter showed the willingness of those three colored pastors to come over to the Missouri Synod. It had been written early in January, 1891. The Mission Board gave this matter due consideration and finally resolved to send a committee to North Carolina to visit the pastors of the Alpha Synod in order to examine their doctrinal position and find out whether the Board could with a good conscience jointly carry on colored mission-work with them.

A COMMITTEE IS SENT TO NORTH CAROLINA.

The Mission Board instructed Rev. Bakke and Rev. Burgdorf, of New Orleans, and Rev. D. H. Schoof, of Meherrin, to repair to North Carolina for the purpose of investigating the matter. They left for the Old North State early in April, about three months after Phifer's letter had been received. Late at night the committee had a conference with Revs. Holt, Clapp, and Phifer in a cabin which belonged to an acquaintance of Holt in Burlington. The conference lasted till the wee small hours in the morning. "Easy catechetical questions were put to the three preachers, but only a few were correctly answered. The theological examination was not satisfactory to the committee; but it saw in the field a door which the Lord had opened, hoped that in the course of time the preachers might be utilized, and advised the Board to take charge of the field, provided a man could be found who would instruct the preachers and superintend the mission." The venerable Rev. Halman, of Spartanburg, S. C., assured the writer several years ago that his synod was glad the Synodical Conference took the work in North Carolina under its care. "We did not have the money," he said. Rev. Halman was president of the North Carolina Synod.

BAKKE IS TRANSFERRED TO CONCORD.

When the Board had considered the report of its committee, it resolved to ask the Board of Distribution to assign two of the graduates that year, 1891, to our Colored Missions, one of whom was to be sent to North Carolina. When this plan failed, Rev. Bakke was asked to move to the new field.

Rev. Bakke arrived in Concord with his family September 18. He found a congregation of 40 baptized members, 20 of whom were also confirmed. In 1883 Rev. Koonts and his members had bought an old frame building, which had first been used as a store and then as the city post-office. One part of this building served as parsonage, the other as church and school. In this room the new minister was introduced by

Rev. Phifer on Sunday, September 20, 1891. Phifer selected a text which might do service for his farewell remarks — he had supplied the congregation with the means of grace after the death of Koonts — and at the same time serve as a text on which he could base his sermon by which he introduced his successor. He selected Acts 20, 29: "For I know this, that after my departing shall grievous wolves enter in among you, not sparing the flock." When Bakke heard his predecessor read these words,

Grace Church, Concord, N. C.
Erected in 1893.

he was not exactly comforted; "but, fortunately for the new missionary, Phifer, as is often the case with colored preachers, did not enter into any explanation of the text."

THE CONCORD SCHOOL IS OPENED.

When Rev. Koonts died, his school in Concord was closed. The new missionary opened it again in October, 1891, and taught it till December, 1893, when Teacher E. Rolf took charge of it. Rolf conducted the school with ability and success for seven years. In 1895 a new school was built. About two years previous to this the present church was erected. It has a seating capacity of 300. Church and school are on East Corbin St., in the heart of the beautiful city of Concord.

PASTORS OF GRACE, CONCORD.

At the end of September, 1898, Rev. Bakke was transferred to Charlotte, N. C. He was succeeded by the theological candidate John Philip Schmidt (Smith), who served the Concord congregation from September 4,

James Spencer.
Died aged 123 years.

1898, to September 12, 1909, when he ordained and installed the theological candidate Henry C. Messerli, who served about three years. His successor, the theological candidate Walter George Schwehn, was installed August 31, 1913. Rev. Schwehn installed his successor, the theological candidate Paul D. Lehman, a graduate of Immanuel Lutheran College at Greensboro, October 3, 1920. Rev. Lehman, a native of Mansura, La., was the first colored pastor of Grace Church. When he had been transferred to our Alabama Luther College in Selma in June, 1923, the present pastor, Rev. Melvin Holsten, became his successor, September 16, 1923. Grace is our largest congregation in the Southeastern Field.

"UNCLE" JAMES SPENCER.

February 9, 1925, Grace Church at Concord lost its oldest member, James Spencer, who was probably the oldest Lutheran in the world, having reached the remarkable age of at least 123 years. Having had a harsh master, he was not permitted to attend divine services; so he stood near the church windows in the darkness of night, listening to the singing and learning such songs as "When I Can Read My Title Clear." He remembered these hymns to the end of his life. "Uncle" James made the acquaintance of Rev. Koonts in Concord and joined his church. He remained a Lutheran to his dying day. Shortly before his death he said to Pastor Holsten: "I am afraid I have forgotten all I once knew. But I know that Jesus is my Savior; and if I believe in Him, I am saved." He fell asleep in Jesus early on Monday morning, February 9, 1925.

A REMARKABLE SEXTON.

Grace Church in Concord has a sexton with an unusual record. He has held the position of sexton since the year 1892; and in all these years he has never failed to be on duty a single Sunday. The punctuality with which he rings the church-bell is the talk of the neighborhood. He does his work free of charge, as a labor of love. His name is *Isaac Lucius Glover.* "Ike" was born July 15, 1871, at Concord. He joined Grace Church under Rev. Koonts and has been a faithful member all these years. Rev. Messerli taught him to play the pipe-organ; and whenever the organist cannot serve, he presides at the organ. He has made his home in the church, occupying the room in the rear. He is a diligent and daily student of the Bible and has devotion every day. He also teaches in the Sunday-school. Isaac has stored his mind and heart with many precious treasures of the divine Word. Rev. Holsten, his pastor, says: "Isaac Glover is a wonderful witness for Christ. He takes tracts to the cotton-mill in which he is employed and gives them to the colored people. He is by nature somewhat timid and shy; yet he is not afraid to confess his faith. Several years ago, during the noon hour in the cotton-mill, he bore witness for Christ in the presence of his fellow-laborers. The white foreman came and listened and finally asked him, 'To what church do you belong?' Isaac answered, 'I am a strict Missouri Lutheran.' His questioner remarked with some satisfaction, 'I thought so. I am a Lutheran too. Only a Lutheran can talk like that.' "

OUR CHURCHES IN THE CAROLINAS.

1. *Grace, Greensboro,* Guilford Co., N. C. Begun the end of November, 1893, by Rev. F. Herman Meyer. Property: Chapel-school. Value: $8,000. Missionary: Rev. Wiley H. Lash, since October 4, 1923.

2. *Luther Memorial, Greensboro.* Begun in 1924, by Prof. Hans Naether.

3. *Mission at Pomona,* near Greensboro. Begun in 1926, by Prof. Hans Naether.

4. *Trinity, Elon College,* Alamance Co., eighteen miles east of Greensboro. Begun by Rev. Samuel Holt, before 1876, at Springdale. Property: Chapel and 1½ acres of land. Value: $600. Missionary: Rev. W. H. Lash, since October 4, 1923.

5. *St. Mark's, Winston-Salem,* Forsyth County, twenty-nine miles west of Greensboro. Begun by Rev. R. Otho L. Lynn, in September, 1913. Property: A building site. Value: $1,526. Missionary: Rev. Jesse A. Hunt, since February 12, 1921.

6. *St. Luke's, High Point,* Guilford Co., fifteen miles southwest of Greensboro. Begun by Rev. N. J. Bakke, 1908. Property: Chapel. Value: $3,000. Missionary: Prof. W. H. Beck of Immanuel Lutheran College, since October 10, 1926.

7. *St. John's, Salisbury,* Rowan Co., thirty-seven miles southwest of High Point. Begun by Rev. F. Herman Meyer, August, 1895. Property: Church and school. Value: $10,000. Missionary: Rev. Carrington R. March, since July 1, 1923.

8. *Mount Olive,* Catawba Co., thirty-eight miles west of Salisbury. Begun by Rev. N. J. Bakke, 1895. Property: Chapel and an acre of land. Value: $650. Missionary: Rev. C. R. March, since January 1, 1924.

9. *Bethel, Conover,* Catawba Co., twelve miles west of Catawba. Begun by Rev. George Schutes, 1904. Property: Chapel. Value: $500. Missionary: Rev. C. R. March, since January 1, 1924.

10. *Mount Zion, Bostian Cross Roads,* Rowan Co., six miles southeast of Salisbury. Begun by Rev. Geo. Schutes, 1904. Property: Chapel and an acre of land. Value: $1,000. Missionary: Rev. J. E. Shufelt, since January 1, 1924.

11. *Concordia, Rockwell,* Rowan Co., six miles east of Bostian Cross Roads. Begun by Rev. N. J. Bakke in the spring of 1893. Property: A chapel-school and an acre of land. Value: $1,200. Missionary: Rev. J. E. Shufelt, since January 1, 1924.

12. *Zion, Gold Hill,* Rowan Co., fifteen miles southeast of Salisbury. Begun by Rev. N. J. Bakke in the summer of 1893. Property: Chapel. Value: $1,000. Missionary: Rev. J. E. Shufelt, since January 1, 1924.

13. *Mount Calvary, near Kannapolis,* Cabarrus Co. Begun by Rev. John Philip Smith, 1902. Property: A chapel-school and two acres of land. Value: $3,000. Missionary: Superintendent Frank D. Alston, since July 1, 1919.

14. *Grace, Concord,* Cabarrus Co. Begun by Rev. David J. Koonts, 1883. Property: Church and school. Value: $20,000. Missionary: Rev. Melvin Holsten, since September 16, 1923.

15. *Immanuel, Shankletown,* a suburb of Concord. Organized by Rev. Walter G. Schwehn, September 5, 1919. Property: Chapel. Value: $1,500. Missionary: Rev. M. Holsten, since September 16, 1923.

16. *Mount Calvary, Mount Pleasant,* Cabarrus Co., nine miles east of Concord. Begun by Rev. N. J. Bakke in the winter of 1893. Property: Chapel, parsonage, and 1⅛ acres of land. Value: $4,500. Missionary: Rev. Frederick Hiram Foard, since September 14, 1926.

17. *St. Peter's, Drys Schoolhouse,* Cabarrus Co., six miles southeast of Concord. Begun by Rev. N. J. Bakke, 1897. Property: Chapel and 2½ acres of land. Value: $1,000. Missionary: Rev. F. H. Foard, since September 14, 1926.

18. *Bethlehem, Monroe,* Union Co., twenty-five miles southeast of Charlotte. Begun by Rev. N. J. Bakke at the beginning of 1900. Property:

Church and Parsonage, Mount Pleasant, N. C.

Chapel. Value: $2,500. Missionary: Rev. F. H. Foard, since September 14, 1926.

19. *St. Paul's, Charlotte,* Mecklenburg Co. Begun by Rev. W. Philo Phifer in 1889. Property: Chapel-school and parsonage. Value: $8,500. Missionary: Rev. John W. Fuller, since August 9, 1925.

20. *Mount Zion, Charlotte.* Begun by Rev. W. Philo Phifer in January, 1896. Property: Chapel. Value: $4,500. Missionary: Rev. J. W. Fuller, since August 9, 1925.

21. *Bethel, Greenville,* in the northwestern part of Charlotte. Begun by Rev. John McDavid, September 4, 1911. Property: Chapel. Value: $2,500. Missionary: Rev. J. W. Fuller, since August 9, 1925.

22. *St. James's, Southern Pines,* Moore Co., 105 miles east of Charlotte. Begun by Rev. N. J. Bakke early in 1898. Value of lot and chapel: $2,500. The chapel is a gift of Holy Cross Congregation in Saginaw, Mich. Missionary: Rev. J. A. Hunt, since August 25, 1926.

23. *St. Luke's, Spartanburg,* South Carolina, seventy-five miles southwest of Charlotte, N. C. Begun by Rev. John McDavid, November 23,

1913. Value of chapel-school: $5,000. Missionary: Rev. Gustavus Roberts, since August 2, 1925.

The congregations in the Carolinas have a total of 1,328 baptized members. The largest membership we find in Grace at Concord.

Our Pastors and Professors in the Southeastern Field, 1926.

Left to right: P. Trumpoldt, Philadelphia; L. G. Dorpat, Meherrin, Va.; John Alston, Atlanta; J. A. Hunt, Winston-Salem; Superintendent J. P. Smith, Greensboro; J. E. Shufelt, Rockwell; G. Roberts, Spartanburg; Prof. F. C. Lankenau, Greensboro; Frank Alston, Kannapolis; Prof. Dr. H. Nau, Greensboro; Wm. Hill, Yonkers, N. Y.; Prof. W. H. Beck, Greensboro; Melvin Holsten, Concord; W. H. Lash, Greensboro; F. Foard, Monroe, N. C.; C. R. March, Salisbury.
(Prof. Wm. Kampschmidt is not on the picture.)

OTHER CHURCHES IN THE SOUTHEASTERN FIELD.

The Southeastern Field includes not only the Carolinas, but also the States of Georgia, Virginia, Pennsylvania, and New York.

1. *St. Mark's, Atlanta, Ga.* Begun by Rev. N. J. Bakke, November 7, 1913. Rev. August Burgdorf had worked in Atlanta from May to December, 1896. Property: A chapel, school, and house. Value: $12,000. Missionary: Rev. Isaac John Alston, since January 1, 1918.

2. *St. Matthew's, Meherrin, Va.* Begun by Rev. W. R. Buehler, April, 1883. Property: Thirty acres of land, a church-school, and a parsonage. Value: $4,500. Missionary: Rev. Lawrence G. Dorpat, since November 18, 1920.

3. *St. Philip's, Philadelphia, Pa.* Begun by city missionary Emil Polzin, 1918. The De Loach family, which had belonged to Bethlehem in New Orleans, moved to Philadelphia in 1918. After their arrival there they visited various Lutheran churches. Two pastors treated them nicely, promising to begin a mission for colored people. However, the seekers noticed that they did not belong to the Missouri Synod and so continued their search until they found "their" church. What a splendid example for Lutherans

Rev. McDavid and His Los Angeles Church.

moving to other cities! Property: Three buildings. Value: $10,000. Missionary: Rev. Paul Trumpoldt, since August 3, 1924.

4. *Bethany, Yonkers, N. Y.* Begun by Rev. Alexander von Schlichten, 1901 and 1907. Property: A building site, valued at $3,000. The congregation is kindly permitted to worship in the parish house of the white congregation. Missionary: Rev. William O. Hill, since March 9, 1911.

CONGREGATIONS IN ISOLATED PLACES.

1. *St. Paul's, Little Rock, Ark.* Begun by Rev. J. F. Doescher, November, 1877. Missionary: Rev. Ad. H. Poppe. He preaches to the members in the home of Mrs. Bosley.

2. *Holy Trinity, Springfield, Ill.* Begun by Prof. Henry Wyneken, December, 1881, and again in November, 1886. Property: Church, school, and parsonage. Value: $10,000. Missionary: Rev. Andrew Schulze, since August 17, 1924.

3. *Grace, Jacksonville, Ill.* Begun by Rev. A. Schulze, January 14, 1925. Property: A portable chapel, valued at $500. Missionary: Rev. A. Schulze.

4. *St. Philip's, Chicago, Ill.* Begun by Rev. M. N. Carter, March 2, 1924. Property: Chapel-parsonage, valued at $25,000. Missionary: Rev. M. N. Carter.

5. *Immanuel, Cincinnati, O.* Begun by Rev. George Kase on Sunday afternoon, September 10, 1922, with four listeners in the home of Thomas and Mary Livingstone, 706 Betts St. Property: Chapel, belonging to the Federation of Lutheran Churches in Cincinnati. Value: $10,000. Missionary: Rev. Geo. Kase.

6. *Grace, St. Louis, Mo.* Begun by Rev. Lucius Thalley, November 8, 1903, at 1008 High St. Property: School. Value: $10,000. Missionary-teacher: Rev. G. L. Kroenk, since June 30, 1923.

7. *St. Philip's, St. Louis, Mo.* Begun by Rev. Paul E. Gose, May 8, 1927, the day on which the church was dedicated. Value of church: $25,000. Missionary: Rev. P. E. Gose.

8. *St. Paul's, Los Angeles, Cal.* The work was begun by Rev. Walter F. Troeger in Santa Monica and by Rev. J. W. Theiss in Los Angeles, 1919, with Lutherans who moved to these cities from New Orleans. Property: Chapel, valued at $8,000. Missionary: Rev. John McDavid, since September 13, 1925.

9. *Mount Zion, Oakland, Cal.* Begun by Rev. J. McDavid, 1926.

These churches at isolated places have a total of about 430 members.

IX. God's Word and Luther's Doctrine Pure in the Black Belt of Alabama.

On his tour of exploration Rev. Doescher also visited Mobile, where he remained two weeks and established a Sunday-school. In December, 1881, the station was closed because it seemed to be unpromising. For about thirty-four years the 900,000 colored people in the State of Alabama had no opportunity to hear the everlasting Gospel which had been brought to light again by the great Reformer, Doctor Martin Luther. Then the unexpected cry came from Alabama, "Come over and help us!"

WHAT THE COTTON BOLL-WEEVIL HAD TO DO WITH IT.

In the "Cotton State" educational opportunities for colored children were deplorable. Many of the schools for colored children are private schools. Such a private school was opened at Rosebud, in Wilcox County, by Teacher Rosa J. Young in 1912.

Miss Rosa Young was born May 14, 1890, at Rosebud. Her father was a Methodist circuit rider for about twenty years. She received her education in the elementary school and at Payne University in Selma, Ala. After her graduation the people at Rosebud requested her to open a private school for the children of the community. She began in 1912 with seven pupils, with whom she met in an old hall, where the cattle went for shelter at night. Having consulted the white people of the neighborhood and received their consent, as well as their promise to lend

Rosa J. Young.

financial assistance, she bought five acres of timber land on a hill and erected a frame schoolhouse. Thus was established *The Rosebud Literary and Industrial School.* Later she also began to erect a chapel adjoining the schoolhouse; however, lack of funds prevented the completion of the chapel. The school was soon crowded. It had an enrolment of 215, and two additional teachers had to be employed. The large girls were instructed in sewing and cooking.

In 1914 the cotton boll-weevil invaded Wilcox County and brought along hard times. The two assistant teachers at Rosebud had to be dismissed. This left the principal alone with more than 100 children. She barely eked out an existence, living on the little which the poor parents of the pupils were able to contribute. Not wishing to lose the school, which was so sorely needed, the trustees appealed for help to the Methodist Church, to which many in that part of the country belonged. However, they met with a refusal. So the board of trustees authorized the principal to offer the school to any Protestant denomination that would promise to conduct it in the interest

Booker T. Washington.

of the colored children. She wrote for advice to the great educator, leader, and counselor of her people, Booker T. Washington, at Tuskegee Institute in Macon County, Ala. Knowing of the educational work of the Synodical Conference among the colored people and having had some correspondence with the writer of this book, the distinguished educator at Tuskegee sent the writer's name and address to Miss Young, advising her to apply in her need to the Lutheran Church. This favor was probably one of Dr. Washington's last acts of kindness, for several weeks later he died.

AN UNEXPECTED LETTER.

Neenah, Ala., October 27, 1915.

Rev. C. F. Drewes,
St. Louis, Mo.

DEAR FRIEND: —

I am writing you concerning a school I have organized. I began teaching here in 1912 with seven pupils in an old hall, where the cattle went for shelter. Since then I have bought [with money collected in the community] five acres of land and erected a four-room schoolhouse thereon beside our chapel, which we are working on now; bought 45 seats, 5 heaters, 1 school bell, 1 sewing-machine, 1 piano, a nice collection of useful books, and 150 New Testaments for our Bible-training Department.

I am writing to see if your Conference will take our school under its auspices. If you will take our school under your auspices, we will give you the land, the school-building, and all its contents to start with. If you cannot take our school, I beg the privilege to appeal to you to give us a donation to help us finish our new chapel. No matter how little, any amount will be cheerfully and thankfully received.

This school is located near the center of Wilcox County, twelve miles from the county-seat, fifty-four miles from Selma, Ala., two miles from the L. and N. Railroad, amid 1,500 colored people. The region is very friendly; both white and colored are interested in this school. I hope you will see your way clear to aid us.

Yours humbly,

ROSA J. YOUNG.

THE APPEAL FROM ALABAMA IS INVESTIGATED.

This letter sounded different from other letters of the kind that come to the writer's desk from time to time. He therefore resolved to have the matter investigated. Accordingly, he instructed the then Field Secretary, Rev. N. J. Bakke, to look into the matter and to report. The Field Secretary was at Rosebud from December 17 to 21. Having heard the Field Secretary's report, the writer called a special meeting of the Mission Board for the afternoon of January 3, 1916, to consider the question of entering the new field. The writer was reminded of Paul's vision at Troas: "A vision appeared to Paul in the night: There stood a man of Macedonia and prayed him, saying, 'Come over into Macedonia and help us.' And after he had seen the vision, immediately we endeavored to go into Macedonia, assuredly gathering that the Lord had called us for to preach the Gospel unto them." The Mission Board resolved to enter the door of opportunity immediately. It instructed the Field Secretary to return to Alabama as soon as possible and to stay until the work would be well started. Rev. William Harrison Lane, assistant missionary in St. Louis, was told to repair to Rosebud. It was resolved to retain Rosa Young as teacher at a salary of $20 a month.

Rev. Bakke arrived at Rosebud January 13, 1916, and remained there three and a half months. Lane arrived February 6. He taught school and did some of the preaching. Five days after his arrival, Rev. Bakke unfurled the banner of Lutheranism in the Black Belt of Alabama and organized several confirmation classes.

SPIRITUAL DARKNESS IN THE BLACK BELT.

Rev. Bakke said in a letter to the writer: "The ignorance here in all matters is simply beyond measure." Most of the so-called preachers were blind leaders of the blind. Mr. J. Lee Bonner, of Rosebud, said: "Those who belong to the church are not better than those who are without; the ignorant preachers are to blame." And Rosa Young wrote: "The people are poor, very, very ignorant, rough, and untrained. They are superstitious and immoral. The present deplorable condition of my race is due largely to their former training and immoral leaders." The statement made to the writer by a member of our church at Kings Landing, Ala., applies to most preachers in the Black Belt. This member said: "The preachers only preached to get a little salary. This particular preacher charged $10 a sermon. First of all the collection was taken. If it was small, he gave a short sermon. That was good fortune. They did not preach the truth to the people. We were in darkness and would have remained in darkness till death. None of them ever told us: 'Christ is your Savior, who died for your sins. Believe in Him, then you are saved.' On the contrary, they said: 'Go into the swamp or into the cemetery or into the woods at night and pray to get religion.' The children grew up like weeds in the field. The sick and the aged were not visited. I was discouraged and wouldn't want to have anything to do with them any more. I stayed at home on Sundays, prayed, and read the Bible to my family. Then I heard of the Lutheran Church in Selma. Rev. Schmidt came. A white lady said to me, 'For God's sake, do not let this good thing pass by!' . . . There was a man here who wanted to join the local sectarian church. He was asked, 'What have you seen?' He replied, 'Nothing. But I believe that Jesus will save me in my dying hour.' The preacher said, 'Well, I'll baptize you on your faith.' Later this man died. The preacher said in the funeral sermon, 'He has gone to hell because he has seen nothing.' We thank God and the Lutheran Mission for having brought us out of this darkness. The Mission has done great things here, wonderfully great things." The statement of this man agrees with what Booker T. Washington wrote.

BOOKER T. WASHINGTON ON THE SECTARIAN PREACHERS.

Dr. Washington wrote some years ago: "Three-fourths of the Baptist ministers and two-thirds of the Methodists are unfit, either mentally or morally, or both, to preach the Gospel to any one or to attempt to lead any one. With few exceptions, the preaching of the colored ministry is emotional in the highest degree, and the minister considers himself successful in proportion as he is able to set the people in all parts of the congregation to groaning, uttering wild screams, and jumping, finally going into a trance. One of the principal ends sought by most of these ministers is their salary, and to this everything else is made subservient. A large proportion of the church-members are just as ignorant of true Christianity as taught by Christ as any people in Africa or Japan and just as much in need of missionary effort as those in foreign lands."

THE FIRST HARVEST OF SOULS AT ROSEBUD.

On Palm Sunday and Easter Sunday, 1916, 58 persons were baptized and 70 confirmed; most of the latter were men and women. On Easter Day a congregation was organized with 117 baptized members, 70 confirmed members, and 22 voting members. In less than a year the congregation at Rosebud had 187 baptized members and 112 confirmed members. This rich harvest was unprecedented in the annals of our Colored Missions and a promise of what was still to come in the Black Belt of Alabama.

Our Mission at Rosebud soon became favorably known

in all the surrounding country and rapidly extended to other places. The colored sectarian preachers were unable to stop its extension. Delegates came from every direction, asking that the work be begun in their communities. Thus our Church had one opportunity after another to carry the light of the Gospel of Christ into the darkness of ignorance, superstition, and sin.

WHITE FRIENDS OF OUR MISSIONS IN ALABAMA.

Under God, the wonderful success of our faithful missionaries has been due, in a measure, to the kindness and support of our white friends. Mr. and Mrs. J. Lee Bonner at Rosebud,

Mary and Sarah McCants.

the Hon. John T. Dale at Oak Hill, Mr. Dennis Forte, formerly a school director at Buena Vista, Mr. George Cook at Rockwest, Supreme Judge B. M. Miller, and others have supported our work by word and deed. Their support has been of inestimable benefit to our work. God bless these white friends!

TWIN SISTERS AT VREDENBURGH.

Mary and Sarah McCants, twin sisters, lived near Vredenburgh, about fifteen miles south of Rosebud. Although nineteen years of age, they attended Rosa Young's school at Rosebud. They and their teacher were the first to come forward at a church meeting held January 16, 1916, for the purpose of expressing their willingness to receive further instruction in the doctrines of the Lutheran Church.

After their confirmation on Palm Sunday they returned to their home near Vredenburgh. Before leaving school, they were advised and encouraged to start a Sunday-school near Vredenburgh. Their relatives and friends tried hard to persuade the girls to sever their connection with the Lutheran Church and to "come back home," as they put it. They did not succeed.

Before long the two sisters prepared to open a Sunday-school. Their father let them have the old, abandoned log cabin which stood about a mile from their home. They scrubbed it. Then they made seats out of an old wagon body

Old School, Buena Vista.
Our First Church and School.

and scraps of planks, which they carried on their heads from their home to the old cabin.

Friday, the second day of June, Teacher Rosa Young walked all the way from Rosebud to Vredenburgh over dusty, hot, and unknown roads in order to assist the twins in their mission-work and to open a day-school. She said in her report to the writer: "When I reached Vredenburgh the second day of June, late in the afternoon, the girls and their mother were at the old cabin making more seats for the Sunday-school. They shouted for joy."

What a wonderful missionary spirit these twins displayed!

HOW OUR MISSION CAME TO BUENA VISTA.

Teacher James Montgomery, now Rev. Montgomery, had taught the public school at Buena Vista, in Monroe County, eleven years. He had also now and then preached in the Baptist

Church. The news of the new church from the North soon reached his ears. So one Sunday he saddled his mule and rode over to Vredenburgh. What he saw and heard in Rosa's Sunday-school made a favorable impression on him, and he invited her to visit his community and tell the people of this new church. She went over August 20, and on the following evening spoke to a packed house in a local church. Montgomery and several of the better class of people requested that Lutheran mission-work be begun at Buena Vista. Their request was granted. Montgomery rode to Oak Hill every Saturday, a distance of eighteen miles, and took religious instruction from Rev. Bakke. November 14, 1920, he was ordained to the Lutheran ministry.

Our Mission Ford on a Road in Alabama.

HOW OUR CHURCH CAME TO TINELA.

About nine miles southwest of Vredenburgh is a place called Tinela. September 18, 1916, Rosa Young was sent to see a white lady, Mrs. Cannon, at Tinela about buying a plot of land for the church at Vredenburgh. She showed the white lady a letter of recommendation from Mr. J. Lee Bonner at Rosebud in which he spoke highly of the colored Lutheran church and school at Rosebud. During the conversation our teacher showed Mrs. Cannon one of our expositions of Luther's Catechism and explained several passages to her and her daughter. They were pleased; and Mrs. Cannon began to tell Rosa about the sad condition of the colored people at Tinela and expressed the belief that such a mission would be a great help to the people there. She also asked Rosa to see if anything could be done. At first she declined, saying that she had not been sent to Tinela to do mission-work. However, Mrs. Cannon insisted that she at least see some of the colored people before leaving and gave her the names of some. The temptation was too strong for her to resist. The parties whom she saw made a date with her to come back to Tinela and to speak to the people.

Rosa Young went back to Tinela and held a meeting in a local church October 15, and again Sunday, November 12. A Sunday-school was begun by a certain J. C. Bradford. Rev. Bakke went there two weeks later. He sent Rev. Lynn to Tinela, who preached the first Lutheran sermon ever heard in that community. However, the impressions gained by Revs. Bakke and Lynn were unfavorable; and so the former ordered Rosa to go to Tinela and collect the books.

Rosa came to Tinela the last day of the year. When she

In This Log Hut the Work was Begun at Tinela.

arrived, she found the people conducting a Sunday-school. All rejoiced to see her. Their rejoicing was so great that she hated to tell them what she had really come for. When all had been dismissed after Sunday-school, she called back Bradford, Buster Lee, and Carrie Williamson and told them what she had come for. "Oh, no; no; no!" they cried. "Miss Young, you cannot do that, because there are several people here who really want to join. That is not right. You-all ought to give Tinela a chance." They called the crowd back and told them what Miss Young had come for. The crowd shouted: "No; no; no! Give Tinela a chance." Then a meeting was appointed for the next day. She told them to be sure to bring all the books; for if she found no prospects for a mission, she would be compelled to "call off."

WHAT HAPPENED AT TINELA ON NEW YEAR'S DAY.

The next day, January 1, 1917, a large crowd turned out. After a song and the Lord's Prayer our teacher gave a talk to the people and then bade them express their opinion and ask any question. Fate Pryear and family, William Burgess and family, and John Davis and family said they wanted to join the church and take instruction. Several others wanted to stay with the Sunday-school.

Rosa pointed out to Bradford and the others that it was proper that those who showed themselves willing to join the church should be at the head of the Sunday-school. She told them that one could not represent a thing well unless one belonged to it. They all agreed; and so she turned over the books to Fate Pryear. They called their Sunday-school Mount Olive. — The congregation at Tinela is a fine, faithful flock. Professor Lynn, their former pastor, says: "In spite of the inadequacy of their place of worship, the ridicule of friends and neighbors, and what, at times, seemed a forlorn hope of ever obtaining a chapel, the members of Mount Olive clung to the confession of the Lutheran Church with a tenacity born of faith and a true love for God and His pure Word."

REV. BAKKE IS TRANSFERRED TO ALABAMA.

Rev. Bakke had left Alabama after three and a half months, in May, 1916. Seeing that the Lord was opening the door of missionary opportunities in Alabama wider and wider, the Mission Board resolved, August 10, 1916, to call Field Secretary Bakke as Superintendent of the new and promising field. He accepted the call and moved to Oak Hill, Ala., arriving there with his family September 25 and remaining in the Black Belt till October 3, 1920. — During our first year in Alabama, 1916, work was begun also at Tilden, Dallas County, and at Possum Bend and Midway, Wilcox County. Early in 1917 the ninth mission-station was begun in Alabama.

MARIE DAVIDSON AT MIDWAY.

When the writer visited the station at Midway the first time on Friday, May 15, 1917, three months after the school at that place had been opened by Teacher Rosa Young, about 200 people came out to the meeting. A little girl, who was exactly three years and three months old, was pointed out to him with the remark, "That little girl knows something of the Catechism too." Before leaving, I called the little child to me and asked her, "Little girl, what do you know of the Catechism?" She folded her fat little hands and recited the Lord's

The Old Church at Midway.
The Property of Supreme Judge Miller.

Prayer without a mistake. Wonderful! But that was not all. Without stopping she recited the entire Second Article of the Creed with Luther's beautiful explanation. Marvelous!

About eight years later, September 25, 1925, the writer visited the congregation at Midway. He was anxious to see

The New Church at Midway. Cost, $2,200.
Albert Woelfle Memorial.

little Marie; but her father informed him that she had been left at home to mind her four-months-old little brother Melvin Holsten Davidson. After the services the writer requested Superintendent George A. Schmidt to take him to the Davidson home. Leaving the main road, we turned into a field and soon lost our way in the darkness and the high weeds. After a while we reached the home. It stands close to the Alabama River, in a lonely spot. It was night, between ten and eleven o'clock. Two barking dogs came running towards the Ford. We stopped. Presently the cabin door was opened slightly. Marie was carefully looking to see who was there. Then she came out, carrying her baby brother on her arm. I said to her, "Hello, Marie! I bet you don't know who I am." "Yes, sir; you are Rev. Drewes from St. Louis," came her reply. Then I asked, "Marie, weren't you afraid to stay here all alone so late with your little brother? Oh, these two dogs protected you." "Yes, and God too," the child added. Oh, the faith and trust in God shown by little Marie! She had learned in the Lutheran mission-school: "I believe that God defends me against all danger and guards and protects me from all evil."

Superintendent G. A. Schmidt.

REV. GEORGE A. SCHMIDT IS SENT TO ALABAMA.

The rapid growth of our Colored Missions in Alabama necessitated much speaking, traveling, buying of building sites and building material, supervision of construction, and so forth. All this work exceeded the strength and time of Superintendent Bakke. He needed help. So the Mission Board transferred Rev. George A. Schmidt from St. Louis to Alabama, making him superintendent of mission-schools and mission-property.

Rev. Schmidt is a native of Chicago. He was born November 26, 1891, attended St. Stephen's School, Concordia College in Milwaukee, and Concordia College in Fort Wayne, and graduated from Concordia Theological Seminary in

St. Louis in June, 1914. After his graduation he accepted a call to our Colored Missions in St. Louis and Springfield, where he proved himself a capable, faithful, and successful worker in the Lord's vineyard. The St. Louis Mission doubled its membership during Rev. Schmidt's pastorate.

He arrived in the Black Belt October 1, 1917, and within the short period of six months he supervised the erection of five buildings besides visiting the schools and serving two congregations. In October, 1920, Rev. Schmidt succeeded Rev. Bakke as superintendent. His increasing age, in particular, induced the Synodical Conference to relieve Rev. Bakke of the arduous duties of the trying position in 1920 and to give him the more pleasant office of Publicity Secretary. The phenomenal growth of our Colored Lutheran Church in Alabama is due largely, under God, to the tireless, conscientious, and efficient work of Superintendent Schmidt. In his modesty he gives most of the credit to others.

At the end of 1926 our Alabama Field had 27 congregations and 2 preaching-places, with 1,789 baptized members, of whom 996 were communicant members. The 27 day-schools had 1,466 pupils enrolled. The contributions during 1926 amounted to $9,312.99.

WHAT HAS BEEN DONE IN ALABAMA.

Superintendent Schmidt writes: "Much has been done to bring joy and happiness into the homes of the people living near our churches. Old and young into whose ears and hearts the Word of God has been sounded, rejoice in the knowledge, a saving knowledge of a loving Savior, who died for their sins on the cross. Though the Lord has blessed our poor, weak, and faulty efforts beyond expectation in the upbuilding of our Lutheran Zion, we have reached *comparatively* few people. There is still much land to be possessed, there are still hundreds and thousands of cabins which are poor, dark, and void. Oh, for men and women who would assist in the work of reaching out a helping hand to those dying in their sins!"

LIST OF CONGREGATIONS IN THE BLACK BELT.

1. *Christ, Rosebud,* Wilcox County. Begun by Rev. N. J. Bakke, January 13, 1916. Property: Chapel-school and parsonage; five acres of land. Value: About $2,000. A new chapel has been erected during this year of jubilee. Missionary: Rev. Walter F. Carlson, since October, 1926.

2. *St. Paul's, Oak Hill,* Wilcox Co. Begun by Rev. Bakke, April 15, 1916. Property: Ten acres of land, chapel-school, and parsonage. Value: $4,000. Missionary: Rev. W. F. Carlson, since October, 1926.

3. *Gethsemane, Hamburg,* Wilcox Co. Begun by Rosa Young in the summer of 1924. Property: 1¾ acres of land and a chapel-school, the present of a Christian lady in Wisconsin. Value: $1,000. Missionary: Rev. W. F. Carlson, since October, 1926.

4. *St. Mark's, Ackerville,* Wilcox Co. Begun by Rev. John Thompson, October, 1926. No property. Missionary: Rev. J. Thompson.

5. *Holy Cross, Camden,* Wilcox Co. Begun by Rev. E. A. Westcott, August 17, 1924. No property. Missionary: Rev. Charles D. Peay, since October, 1926.

6. *Our Savior, Possum Bend,* Wilcox Co. Begun by Rev. N. J. Bakke, Thanksgiving Day, 1916. Property: Five acres of land and a chapel-school. Value: $1,000. Missionary: Rev. C. D. Peay, since October, 1926.

7. *Our Redeemer, Longmile,* Wilcox Co. Begun by Superintendent Geo. A. Schmidt, February 19, 1922. Property: Four acres of land and a chapel-school. Value: $1,200. Missionary: Rev. Eugene Cozart, since October 1, 1926.

8. *St. Andrew's, Vredenburgh,* Wilcox Co. Begun by Mary and Sarah McCants, May, 1916. Property: Five acres of land and a chapel-school. Value: $1,000. Missionary: Rev. E. B. Cozart, since the fall of 1924.

9. *Zion, Taits Place,* Wilcox Co. Begun by Superintendent Schmidt the night of October 7, 1919. Property: Two acres of land, a chapel-school, and a teacherage. Value: $1,500. Missionary: Rev. J. Thompson, since October, 1926.

10. *Bethel, Rockwest,* Wilcox Co. Begun by Superintendent Schmidt, September 25, 1924. Property: Two acres of land and a chapel-school, the gift of a Christian woman in California. Value: $1,000. Missionary: Rev. C. D. Peay, since October, 1926. — This station was opened in response to an urgent appeal for the Lutheran Church and school made by a white man, Mr. Geo. Cook.

11. *Mount Carmel, Midway,* Wilcox Co. Begun by Rev. N. J. Bakke, December 7, 1916. Property: Five acres of land and a chapel-school, donated by the late Albert Woelfle of Nebraska. Value: $3,000. Missionary: Rev. C. D. Peay, since October, 1926.

12. *Bethany, Nyland,* Wilcox Co. Begun by Superintendent Schmidt, February 8, 1918. Property: Two acres of land and a chapel-school. Value: $1,200. Missionary: Rev. James Montgomery, since September 11, 1921.

13. *St. Peter's, Pine Hill,* Wilcox Co. Begun by Rev. J. Montgomery, November 1, 1922. Property: Two acres of land and a chapel-school, the gift of a friend of our Colored Missions who lives in California. Value: $1,000. Missionary: Rev. J. S. Montgomery.

14. *St. Matthew's, Arlington,* Wilcox Co. Begun by Rev. J. Montgomery in November, 1923. Property: One acre of land and a chapel-school, the gift of friends of our Colored Missions living in Courtland, Minn. Value: $1,000. Missionary: Rev. J. S. Montgomery, since November, 1925.

15. *St. Luke's, Lamison,* Wilcox Co. Begun by Superintendent Schmidt, 1925. No property. Missionary: Rev. J. S. Montgomery, since 1926. — (Fifteen churches in Wilcox County.)

16. *Mount Calvary, Tilden,* Dallas Co. Begun by Rev. N. J. Bakke, November 12, 1916. Property: Three acres of land, chapel-school, and parsonage. Value: $5,000. Missionary: Rev. J. Thompson, since August 2, 1925.

17. *Grace, Ingomar,* Dallas Co. Begun by Rev. N. J. Bakke, May 11, 1919. Property: Five acres of land, chapel-school, and teacherage. Value: $1,000. Missionary: Rev. J. Thompson, since August 2, 1925.

18. *Trinity, Selma,* Dallas Co. Begun by Rev. C. D. Peay, July 11, 1920. Services are held in the chapel of our Alabama Luther College. Missionary: Prof. P. D. Lehman, since July 1, 1925.

19. *Hope, Kings Landing,* Dallas Co. Begun by Superintendent Schmidt, January 17, 1924. Property: About two acres of land, bought

Church and School at Possum Bend.
Rough lumber. Such a building costs about $1,000.

by the congregation, a teacherage, and a chapel-school, which was given to the Mission Board by the other congregations in Alabama as "a token of appreciation for the many deeds of love and kindness from our host of supporters. It is to show how deeply we are grateful to God for His blessings which have come to us through the Lutheran Church." Value: $1,200. Missionary: Prof. R. O. L. Lynn, since October, 1926.

20. *St. John's, Joffre* (old Kingston), Autauga Co. Begun by Samuel Ulysses Young in February, 1917. Property: Two acres of land and a chapel-school. Value: $1,000. Missionary: Rev. Paul Weeke, since March 2, 1924.

21. *Bethlehem, Holy Ark,* Autauga Co. Begun by Superintendent Schmidt, January 15, 1922. Property: Two acres of land and a chapel-school. Value: $1,000. Missionary: Rev. Paul Weeke, since March 2, 1924.

22. *Pilgrim, Birmingham.* Begun by Rev. M. N. Carter, July 11, 1920. No property. Missionary: Rev. Wm. T. Eddleman, since October 4, 1925.

23. *Faith, Mobile.* Begun by Rev. R. O. L. Lynn, May 13, 1920. Property: A building site. Value: $2,150. Missionary: Rev. Gustave G. Kreft, since March, 1926.

24. *Ebenezer, Atmore,* Escambia Co. Begun by Superintendent Schmidt, May 29, 1925. Property: A chapel-school, the present of a friend in Brooklyn, N. Y. Value: $2,000. Missionary: Rev. G. G. Kreft, since November, 1925.

25. *Station at Pensacola,* Florida. Begun by Superintendent Schmidt in October, 1924, in the vestry of Immanuel Lutheran Church (white). Missionary: Rev. G. G. Kreft, since March, 1926. This is our only mission-station in Florida.

26. *Mount Olive, Tinela,* Monroe Co., Ala. Begun by Rosa Young, September 18, 1916. Property: Five acres of land and a chapel-school. Value: $1,000. Missionary: Rev. W. F. Carlson, since July, 1923.

27. *St. James's, Buena Vista,* Monroe Co. Begun by Rosa Young in August, 1916. Property: Five acres of land and a chapel-school. Value: $800. Missionary: Rev. E. B. Cozart, since the fall of 1924.

The plan usually followed in Alabama is the T-plan: the chapel in front and in the rear two schoolrooms. As a rule, rough lumber is used, just as it comes from the sawmill.

X. Our Mission-Schools.

After freedom had come to the Negroes, many ex-slaves manifested a great desire to acquire an education. During the dark days of slavery it had been strictly forbidden by law to teach them reading, writing, and arithmetic.

From 1865 to 1870 the Freedmen's Bureau established 4,239 schools for the colored people. The former Slave States did very little for the education of the colored youth until the Negro exodus to the North set in after the World War. Particularly in the rural districts poor equipment and short terms are still the rule. This situation has made our mission-schools most welcome.

The education and training which the youth of our country, including the colored youth, needs is a Christian education and training. Said a prominent Southern Presbyterian preacher in a lecture delivered in New Orleans some years ago: "The colored youth must be brought up in *Christian* schools. Through the public schools the ruin of the colored race only becomes greater."

From the very beginning of our Colored Missions to the present day the Christian day-school has occupied a prominent part on our missionary program. We have forty-eight such schools. The teaching force consists of 19 men and 48 women. Besides these no less than 13 of our pastors teach school five days a week. We believe this is unique and without a parallel in the field of Colored Missions in the United States.

WHAT IS DONE IN THE LUTHERAN MISSION-SCHOOL?

In the morning, school is opened with a brief devotion; a hymn is sung, and the Lord's Prayer and perhaps the Apostles' Creed are spoken by the entire school. Thus the work of the day is begun with God. As a rule, the devotional exercises are followed by a lesson in religion: A Bible-story is related, and questions on the story are asked by the teacher. In the Catechism lesson on the following day a simple explanation of Luther's Small Catechism is used as text-book. This explanation has been especially written for our mission-schools by the writer of this book. In the religious hour, parts of the Small Catechism, prayers, and hymns which have been memorized by the pupils are recited.

In Our Christian Schools the Savior Blesses Children.
Between 3,000 and 4,000 pupils attend our 48 mission-schools.

The lesson in religion ended, secular branches are taken up till the noon hour. Before school is dismissed at noon, the pupils repeat a prayer in which they ask the Lord to bless their food. When school takes up again, they repeat a prayer, in which they return thanks to the Giver of every good and perfect gift. At the close of school in the afternoon a hymn is sung and a prayer spoken. Thus the Lutheran mission-school is opened and closed with song and prayer. Attention is given also to practising sacred as well as secular songs. Children love to sing. It is a pleasure to hear them sing our good old Lutheran hymns in school and church, at home, and at work. The Lutheran Church is a singing Church; this is particularly true of our colored Lutheran Church.

"A VERY CREDITABLE WORK."

The chief aim and purpose of our mission-schools is to impart to the pupils a treasure of religious truths, to make them wise unto salvation, and to qualify them to be good citizens, good men and women. However, the secular branches, such as reading, writing, number work, and so forth, are by no means neglected. That our schools do really creditable work is admitted even by their enemies. During the World War false reports were spread with regard to our work by evilly disposed or, at least, sadly misinformed men and women. In order to investigate these rumors, a great New York newspaper instructed a staff correspondent to look into the matter. This is what the correspondent said of our schools in his published report: "They have done, first and last, no doubt, a very creditable work."

A NURSERY AND FEEDER OF THE CHURCH.

In our Christian day-schools hundreds upon thousands of colored boys and girls have learned to know their Savior and have been brought into the sheepfold of Christ during the half century of our mission-work. Many of these boys and girls would otherwise have grown up as heathen.

Of course, not all who attended our schools have joined our Church. Many are seemingly lost to us. Their parents or other close relatives often throw obstacles in the way of the children when they wish to be confirmed. Yet hundreds of such children are and remain Lutherans at heart or join our Church when they become of age. We are happy to know and say that such parents and other relatives do not always succeed in their opposition, as may be seen from a few examples. We have already related the example of Louis Thomas. Here is another instance: —

LOYAL IN SPITE OF PERSECUTION.

Rev. F. J. Lankenau has told this story: I was once called to a sick girl. This girl had formerly attended our school, but was taken away from us and sent to a Roman Catholic priest to receive religious instruction, whereupon she was confirmed by him. Being but a student at that time, I took Rev. Burgdorf along. The father, having heard that we were coming, was furious. He received us at the gate with a drawn knife in his hand, refusing us admittance. After some parleying, however, we succeeded in entering the house where the girl lay. She was glad to see us. We had a long conversation, which was interrupted, however, by several women, who requested us to go into the adjoining room for a little while because the patient needed rest. As the request seemed so reasonable, we

Our St. Louis Mission School.

Forty-one of these pupils were baptized by Rev. Kroenk, in 1926.

went into the adjoining room. Scarcely, however, had the door of the sick-room closed behind us, when we heard the opening of the gate and the tinkling of a little bell — the Roman priest

School "Orchestra," Napoleonville, La.

had been sent for by some one and was just coming, and that was why we had been asked to leave the room.

What were we to do? Should we go home? No, we resolved to stay and await further developments. The priest remained only a few minutes; for the girl told him plainly that she had not sent for him and did not desire his services.

Pupils at Lunch, Tinela, Ala.

When he had left, we returned to the sick-room, continuing our conversation with the patient.

In about two weeks the girl was well again. She promised to come to church regularly. However, Sunday after Sunday passed, and she did not come. Neither was I able to see the girl to learn the cause of her absence. Thus a whole month passed after her recovery. Then, somewhat unexpectedly, an opportunity presented itself to speak to her. I ascertained that her father had forcibly kept her from coming to our church. But seeing the determination of his daughter and probably seeing that his efforts were in vain, he relented. The girl later joined our church, and after several years her mother followed her example. But the strangest thing was that the father himself, having taken sick, sent for me to prepare him for death, and I was able to give him a Lutheran burial.

Two "Students" at Mansura, La.
They intend to become ministers.

A BAD BOY SAVED.

Not all the children who leave the school without joining the Church are really lost. Rev. Theodore Buch was pastor of St. James's at Southern Pines from 1901 to 1903. Like other missionaries, he also taught school. He had to expel one of the boys for being impertinent and wicked. Two years later the boy's mother asked the pastor to come and visit her son.

The missionary found the boy sick unto death. No sooner had he entered than he heard the former bad boy greet him with the words: "Mr. Buch, my trust is all in my Jesus." The boy had heard the story of Jesus and His love in the Lutheran school. At first he despised this wondrous story, but later, in his sickness, it took root in his heart and brought forth fruit unto life everlasting.

THE TEACHING AND TRAINING IN OUR MISSION-SCHOOLS MAKES FOR HONESTY.

Rev. John McDavid, who is not only a good pastor, but also a good teacher, writes: "Once I had to call at a place in Charlotte where one of my members was in service. The young lady had been at this place ever since she left our school. The mistress told me that she was just like one of the family. The pupils of our schools make good servants. They are reliable, honest, and industrious. And this goes a long way in solving the vexed race problem of the South."

AN UNSOLICITED TESTIMONIAL.

A Lutheran pastor who does not belong to our Synodical Conference, having observed our mission-work in the South, sent this unsolicited letter to the writer: —

"Permit me, then, to say, among other things, that the mission to the Negro under the management of your Board is accomplishing more for the Negro, both spiritually and socially, than any other agency. Your insistence on catechization (the very thing that the Negro needs, and the most difficult to accomplish) through the work of your parochial school has been productive of an intelligent confession and profession. This intelligence has made him [the Negro] more stable and consistent. It has made him more valuable to himself and to his fellow-man. I have heard the statement frequently from many of the white folks who know that if you can secure the services of a Lutheran Negro, you will have a good one. Your mission to the Negro is a great and glorious undertaking."

God bless our Lutheran mission-schools among the colored people!

XI. Our White Missionaries.

The first missionaries who were sent to the colored people by our Board were whites, of course. To-day it is different. Of our missionary force of 115, at the beginning of 1927, 27 are white: 2 superintendents, 6 professors, 16 pastors, and 3 teachers.

Many of our white missionaries were men of a high order of intellect, culture, and consecration. In after-years some of them were called by the Lord to large white congregations or placed in high offices of the Church. These missionaries are a band of real heroes. It was their lot to be misunderstood and treated with coldness and contempt by many of the whites. They and their families often suffered social ostracism. At times they were positively persecuted. Think of a highly edu-

Rev. E. Westcott, Selma.

cated young minister and his cultured young wife being refused a house which they wished to rent simply because they have followed the call of the Lord to work among the colored people! Rev. Ed H. Schmidt and his young bride hunted in vain for a house for three weeks; no white landlord would let them have a vacant house. At last the principal of the public school took pity on them and permitted them to live in a small house in the rear of his yard. Many such sad stories could be told.

THE TESTIMONY OF AN EYE-WITNESS.

Mrs. H. C. Monroe, a member of the United Lutheran Church and a prominent missionary writer, visited our mission-field in North Carolina some years ago and then published her findings in a letter published in the *Lutheran Observer*. She said, among other things: "Livingstone is honored over the Christian world for his missionary work in Africa, and Dr. Day is honored all over the Lutheran Church for his missionary work in that same country; yet when a Lutheran missionary, in free and enlightened America, tries to enlighten and lead the colored people to a higher and truer religious life, he often meets with contempt and even scorn. Rev. J. C. Schmidt, at Greensboro, with a highly accomplished wife, has a lonely time. If he were sent to Africa, he would be followed by the love, prayers, and sympathy of the entire Lutheran Church. Letters in the papers would herald his movements; he would be remembered at Christmas; but he and these other devoted men

Rev. M. Dorpat, Meherrin.

seem to have closed the doors of good society behind them in laboring for these poor African people in the South; and amid an isolation which most of us would consider paralyzing they are doing your work and mine for Jesus Christ."

REV. NILS JULES BAKKE.

Rev. Bakke was our third resident missionary. He spent his entire ministerial life in the service of the colored people. Bakke was born September 8, 1852, in the city of Drontheim, Norway, where, in former centuries, the Norwegian kings were crowned. When seventeen years of age, he came to America with his parents. It was his wish to become a minister. So his parents sent him to Luther College at Decorah, Iowa, where he completed his classical course in 1877. He studied three years at Concordia Seminary in St. Louis, graduating June 28, 1880. The faculty of the Seminary recommended him to the Board for Colored Missions as a suitable man. Rev. Buenger, the chairman of the Board, handed him the call as missionary to New Orleans in the Seminary immediately after his final examination. The graduate accepted the call August 17. Sunday, November 7, 1880, he was ordained by Rev. Buenger in Immanuel Church at St. Louis. Two days later he and Miss Concordia Guenther, daughter of Prof. Martin Guenther of Concordia Seminary, were joined in holy wedlock. During the following week they left for New Orleans.

Rev. Paul Trumpoldt,
Philadelphia.

Rev. Bakke labored hard and faithfully for two years in "Sailors' Home" before he was able to confirm two women, Margaret Mosely and Mary C. Wright. He also served St. Paul's. In the summer of 1891, after having worked in New Orleans eleven years, he was transferred to the new field in North Carolina. He was pastor of Grace Church in Concord from September 18, 1891, to September 25, 1898, when the Board transferred him to Charlotte. The following year the

Board intended to send him back to New Orleans and to let Rev. August Burgdorf succeed him in North Carolina. However, the latter was unable to accept the call.

In the fall of 1900 the Mission Board called Rev. Bakke to take preliminary steps towards the opening of a preparatory school for the education and training of colored ministers and teachers. He opened this school March 2, 1903, and was its president for about seven years. In January, 1911, the Mission Board chose him for the newly created office of Field Secretary. It was thought that his impaired health would improve in this new position. He accepted the call and entered upon the discharge of his new duties at the end of the school year 1911. On November 8 of the following year he met with an injury in a runaway and was disabled for seven months. As traveling proved difficult for him, as well as for other reasons, the Mission Board called him as superintendent of the new field in Alabama, in August, 1916. He remained in charge of the new office until, upon the advice of the Board, the Synodical Conference created the office of General Publicity Agent for him, in August, 1920. He left Alabama in October, 1920, moving to Milwaukee. He was suddenly taken seriously ill May 3, 1921, and passed to his eternal reward May 8, at 9.30 A. M., at the age of 68 years and 8 months. He was buried in Wanderers' Rest Cemetery, Milwaukee.

Rev. Bakke was about six feet tall and possessed a strong constitution. He was brave and fearless in the face of threats of bodily violence. He spoke English with somewhat of a Norwegian accent. As a preacher he possessed splendid gifts. His delivery was interesting and at times eloquent. He employed his gifts of both body and mind in our Colored Missions for more than forty years. His former parishioners and students call his memory blessed.

REV. FRANCIS JAMES LANKENAU.

A minister who has spent more than eighteen years of his life in the service of our Colored Missions and still renders great and valuable services to this cause deserves special mention in this jubilee book.

Francis James Lankenau was born in Fort Wayne, Ind., April 26, 1868. His parents were Henry Lankenau and Catherine Schumm. He entered Emmanuel parish school at Fort Wayne at the age of six and attended it till nine. Later he attended the Christian day-school at Schumm, Van Wert Co., O., and at Bingen, Adams Co., Ind. At the latter place his father was his teacher. After his confirmation he attended Fort Wayne College (not Concordia) at intervals for several years. He started out as teacher at the youthful age of only sixteen years. He taught public school at Williams, Ind., three terms. The young teacher took up the private study of law and had made preparations to attend a law school. However, the

Rev. F. J. Lankenau.

late Prof. Rudolph Bischoff, first editor of our *Lutheran Pioneer*, at that time pastor of St. John's at Bingen, persuaded him to take up the study of theology. So he entered Concordia Seminary at Springfield, Ill., in September, 1887. After Teacher Berg's death young Lankenau did supply-work at the following places: for six months in St. Paul's School, New Orleans, from March to August, 1888; for twelve months at Meherrin, Va., August, 1889, to July, 1890; from December, 1890, to March, 1891, at Edinburgh, Ill.

After his graduation in June, 1891, Candidate Lankenau

accepted a call as pastor of Mount Zion and St. Paul's in New Orleans and was ordained and installed by Rev. August Burgdorf in Mount Zion, Sunday, August 23, 1891. He served St. Paul's uninterruptedly till September 6, 1908, and Mount Zion till May 1, 1894, and thereafter during two vacancies. Under his zealous care the membership of St. Paul's increased from 136 to 315. He opened the mission-station at Mansura in March, 1898, and the mission-station at Napoleonville in June, 1905. In September, 1903, he opened Luther College in the vestry of St. Paul's, New Orleans, and served as professor and president till September, 1908, at the same time performing the duties of his pastorate at St. Paul's.

In September, 1908, Rev. Lankenau accepted a call to the congregation at Napoleon, O. Not only the members of his congregation, young and old, but also his colleagues in New Orleans regretted his leaving. Rev. Kramer wrote: "The entire Colored Mission in New Orleans sorrows with Rev. Lankenau's congregation; particularly we young missionaries view his leaving with heavy hearts. He assisted us inexperienced workers with fatherly counsel. Whenever we were at our wits' end, Pastor Lankenau had to help us."

In 1912, the Mission Board chose Rev. Lankenau editor of the *Lutheran Pioneer*. He has ably edited this missionary periodical since January, 1913. From 1921 to 1926 he was Vice-President of the Central District of the Missouri Synod. At the delegate synod held in St. Louis in June, 1926, he was chosen one of the Vice-Presidents of the whole synod. Since 1924 he has been chairman of the Advisory Board of Valparaiso University. He is a quick and clear thinker, a ready writer, an eloquent and convincing speaker. Rev. Lankenau is faithful and zealous in all his undertakings.

JOHN PHILIP SMITH.

This gifted and faithful worker gave his whole ministerial life — about twenty-six years — to the service of our Colored Missions as pastor, professor, president of Immanuel Lutheran College, and superintendent of the Southeastern Field.

After his graduation from the St. Louis Seminary, young Smith accepted a call into our Colored Missions. He was ordained at the convention of the Synodical Conference in Cincinnati, August 14, 1898. Prof. Wm. Dau preached the ordination sermon on Mal. 2, 7. He served the congregations at Concord and Drys Schoolhouse. At the latter place he was installed under the "Holy Oak." In 1902 he organized Mount Calvary Congregation near Kannapolis. When Immanuel Lutheran College was opened in Concord, he assisted to the extent of giving ten periods a week. In December, 1908, the Mission Board called him as professor to Greensboro. He continued to

Prof. J. P. Smith.

serve his two congregations till the fall of the next year, going to Concord every week, a distance of 72 miles. Owing to the health of his wife, he resigned October 1, 1917. He found a lucrative position in Port Huron, Mich. But when the health of Mrs. Smith improved and the call of the Colored Missions came to him again, he accepted the call to Immanuel Lutheran College as professor and president in the summer of 1919. In the summer of 1925 the Board called him as superintendent of the Southeastern Field. His death came after a brief, but painful illness on March 26, 1926. He died at the age of 47 years, 9 months, and 25 days. Smith was always found a faithful servant and performed his various duties with success.

REV. G. M. KRAMER.

There are two missionaries in our Colored Missions who enjoy the distinction of having served one and the same congregation uninterruptedly for a period of twenty years. The one is Rev. John McDavid, the other Rev. G. M. Kramer. Rev. Kramer has received more than one call during this time; but his sympathy for the colored people and his conscientiousness have always constrained him to stay, although this meant personal sacrifice.

Kramer was born September 4, 1882, near Frohna, Perry Co., Mo. His grandparents came over with the Saxon pilgrims in 1838. The kindly, evangelical Pastor Zschoche confirmed him and approached Kramer Senior with the suggestion that he send his son to college. The boy, however, was unwilling. He worked on the farm two years. During this time he heard a missionary sermon on the text: "The harvest, truly, is plenteous, but the laborers are few." This sermon made a deep impression on him; and the following September, 1898, found him at Concordia College in Fort Wayne. Six years later he entered the Seminary in St. Louis. While a student in St. Louis, he taught school in the local colored mission about two and a half months, at the end of 1906 and the beginning of the year 1907. After his graduation in June, 1907, he accepted a call into our Colored Missions. He was ordained and installed in Bethlehem Chapel, New Orleans, August 18, 1907. From October, 1907, to May, 1908, Kramer served the vacant congregation at Napoleonville, eighty-five miles west of New Orleans. During his service of twenty years in Bethlehem five pastors have left Mount Zion, and our willing worker has invariably stepped in to supply the orphaned congregation. In August, 1912, Rev. Kramer reopened the station in Carrollton, a suburb of New Orleans, which had been closed since 1894. Since then he has two congregations under his care and preaches in both every Sunday. Because of his experience, faithfulness, and good judgment the Board, in 1918, chose him as official Visitor for the field in Louisiana. Rev. Kramer is also a contributor to our missionary papers, particularly to the *Missionstaube,* and possesses the gift of writing in an interesting and instructive way.

SOME OF OUR OTHER WHITE MISSIONARIES WHO SERVED LONG.

1. *Rev. George Allenbach* served in Little Rock from November 16, 1884, to August 24, 1890. He is now located in Columbus, O.

2. *Rev. August Burgdorf* served from October 4, 1885, to 1898 in Carrollton, New Orleans (Bethlehem), in Atlanta, Ga., etc. He is now in Chicago.

3. *Rev. K. Kretzschmar,* pastor of Mount Zion, New Orleans, from September 2, 1900, to the spring of 1907. He is now in Fort Smith, Ark.

4. *Rev. Ed Schmidt,* pastor in Napoleonville and New Orleans (St. Paul's) from May 10, 1908, to July 28, 1918 (ten years). He is now pastor in Sheboygan, Wis.

5. *Rev. John C. Schmidt,* pastor in Greensboro, N. C., from September, 1894, to September 1, 1907 (thirteen years). He supervised the erection of Immanuel Lutheran College. Now pastor in California.

6. *Rev. D. H. Schoof,* pastor at Meherrin from September 18, 1890, to October, 1907 (seventeen years). He lives near Janesville, Wis.

7. *Rev. George Schutes,* pastor at Salisbury, N. C., from August 8, 1897, to September 25, 1904. Now pastor at Valparaiso, Ind.

Most of the white pastors stayed only a comparatively short time in our Colored Missions. The resultant numerous vacancies and changes have been detrimental to the growth of our colored Lutheran Church. This was one of the factors which prompted the Mission Board to advocate the establishment of a school of higher learning for the education and training of colored pastors.

XII. Our Schools of Higher Learning.

It is a sound missionary policy to furnish the people who have been gained for Christ and His Church a native ministry. In agreement with this policy the fathers and founders of our Colored Missions from the very beginning planned to educate and train colored ministers. In the plan which the committee submitted to the convention of the Synodical Conference in 1877 it was expressly provided "that indigent, good, and gifted boys who want to devote themselves to mission-work should be supported out of the mission treasury and for the present be trained at one of the institutions of the synods belonging to the Synodical Conference." When Doescher came to Florida on his tour of exploration, in 1878, he expressed the belief that Florida would be a good place for a Negro seminary. During the first quarter century of our Colored Missions this matter of establishing a school of higher learning came up for discussion at many of the conventions of the Synodical Conference.

In 1882 a beginning was made to carry out the plan submitted in 1877. Nathanael L. Burkhalter (born January 13, 1856) entered Concordia at Springfield after Easter. He did not graduate. In September, 1891, Emmanuel Burthlong, a gifted and God-fearing graduate of St. Paul's in New Orleans, entered the Springfield institution. A year later John McDavid, who had been confirmed in Bethlehem, New Orleans, was sent to Springfield. In the fall of 1898 Rev. J. C. Schmidt, of Greensboro, sent Stuart Doswell and Lucius Thalley to the same seminary. Both graduated in 1902. Burthlong died a few months before his graduation. John McDavid is pastor in California. In 1904 James Doswell, a cousin of Stuart, and Wiley H. Lash graduated. Teacher Evan W. Reid graduated from Martin Luther College at New Ulm, Minn., in 1903.

A PETITION FROM IMMANUEL CONFERENCE.

The missionaries in North Carolina and Virginia were firmly convinced that the colored ministers and teachers should be educated and trained on the field, that is, in the South. At the first meeting of Immanuel Conference, February 2—5, 1900, at Concord, they resolved to "petition the Board of Missions to advocate the establishing of a theologico-normal-industrial college for the colored people, so that this much-needed institution may be erected in the near future."

The Board submitted this petition to the Synodical Conference at its meeting in 1900. A lively discussion followed, which led to the adoption of a resolution instructing the Mission Board to have the matter discussed in the *Missionstaube* during the next two years to enable the pastors and congregations throughout the Synodical Conference to become better acquainted with the project. This resolution was carried out. The 1902 convention unanimously resolved to establish, as soon as possible, one or two preparatory schools for the education of colored ministers and teachers.

IMMANUEL LUTHERAN COLLEGE IS OPENED.

Immanuel Conference resolved at its meeting in Concord, in August, 1902, to petition the Mission Board to open a high school temporarily in the school at Concord that fall. Several boys were ready to enter the institution. However, the Mission Board was unable to find a suitable professor. The *Missionstaube* of February, 1903, brought this announcement: "God

Dr. H. Nau, President.

Prof. H. Naether.

Prof. Wm. Kampschmidt.

Prof. W. H. Beck.

Four of Our Professors at Greensboro.

has hitherto not permitted us to find the man who could take the first professorship at this institution. Three times we have called in vain. Dear friends of missions, pray the Lord that He would soon let us find the right man for this important place."

Two months later the announcement was made that Rev. Bakke had declared himself willing to fulfil the wish of the Board to give lessons at the new institution in Concord for the present. March 2, 1903, he opened Immanuel with five boys; later the number increased to eleven. The second story of the schoolhouse in Concord served as dormitory and classroom, and the little two-room frame cottage in the rear of the church was turned into a kitchen and dining-room. Rev. J. P. Smith, the pastor of Grace Church, and his teacher, Henry Persson, assisted the lone professor by teaching two periods a day. The following year (1904) Candidate Frederick Wahlers was called as second professor. He was installed September 12 and served till August 15, 1919, fifteen years.

We shall mention some of the other professors: Prof. J. P. Smith; Prof. Martin Lochner, now professor at River Forest; Prof. H. W. Gross, now pastor at Salem, Oreg.; Prof. Frederick Berg, since June 30, 1911; his son, Albert Berg; Prof. A. E. Kunzmann, now professor in Winfield; Prof. H. N. Wittschen, now at Pelham, N. Y.; Prof. Walter G. Schwehn, now pastor of St. John's at Hannibal, Mo.; Prof. Henry Voltz, now living at Crown Point, Ind.; Prof. Enno Schuelke, now pastor at Ridgeway, N. C.; Prof. Frank C. Lankenau, since the fall of 1921; Prof. J. E. Shufelt; Prof. Wm. Roerig, now in Minneapolis, Minn.; Prof. Theo. Rennegarbe; Prof. Henry Nau, Ph. D., since June, 1925; Prof. Wm. Kampschmidt, since August, 1924; Prof. Walter H. Beck (from the Wisconsin Synod) since 1925; and Prof. Hans Naether, since the fall of 1923.

IMMANUEL LUTHERAN COLLEGE IS MOVED.

At its convention in 1904 the Synodical Conference resolved to educate colored students entirely, in the course of time, at our colored institutions of learning and henceforth to give those who intend to become teachers a full teachers' course; and gifted Christian girls, too, should be admitted to the institutions. The convention appropriated $10,000 to $15,000 for Immanuel. A tract of land comprising about 14½ acres was acquired in the city of Greensboro, and building operations were begun in July, 1905. Expecting the building to be ready for occupancy during the following school-year, the professors and students moved from Concord to Greensboro on September 12,

Our Student-Body in Greensboro, February 15, 1926.

1905. There the institution found a temporary home (four years) in two rented houses belonging to a colored man by the name of Holly. The dedication did not take place till June 2, 1907. The total cost was $28,393.93, almost double the sum appropriated. The debt which was thus incurred was a serious obstacle to the progress of the Colored Missions for a number of years.

The college building is of Mount Airy granite and three stories high. In 1911 a brick-veneer schoolhouse was erected on the college campus at a cost of $3,703.69. It is the gift of the schoolchildren in the Synodical Conference, the same as the schoolhouse in Concord. From the fall of 1919 to the present year the schoolhouse in Greensboro was used as a girls' dormitory. During this year of jubilee a new $50,000 dormitory is being erected. There are three professors' dwellings on the campus. The total value of the plant is approximately $130,000.

THE THREE DEPARTMENTS OF IMMANUEL.

The institution has three departments: 1. *A Senior High School,* which is accredited by the State of North Carolina. 2. *A Normal Department:* Four years in the high school and one year of normal work. 3. *A Theological Seminary.* The course in the seminary is three years. Accordingly, the full course for our ministers is seven years and for our teachers five years.

Superintendent Frank D. Alston and Miss Eliza Johnston were the first graduates from the Normal Department, in June, 1907. The first graduates from the Theological Department were: Rev. John Alston, of Atlanta; Rev. Fred H. Foard, of Monroe, N. C.; Rev. Charles D. Peay, of Selma, Ala. Of the twenty-three colored professors and pastors in our Colored Missions now in our service sixteen are graduates of the Theological Department in Greensboro.

At the convention of the Synodical Conference held at Lockport, N. Y., in August, 1926, the question of general education at our higher institutions of learning was freely and fully discussed. The discussion ended in a unanimous resolution supporting the policy of the Mission Board, which permits the admission of such students also as have not the holy ministry or the teaching profession in view.

Our Theological Students at Greensboro. February, 1926.

Left to right: Frank Thompson, R. Ingram, L. Gauthreaux, F. Vorice, Albert Dominick, C. Malloy, Wilbur Twitty.

LUTHER COLLEGE.

In September, 1903, Rev. F. J. Lankenau opened Luther College in the 10×20 vestry-room of St. Paul's Church in New Orleans. Revs. K. Kretzschmar and J. Kossmann assisted him in the instruction of the students. November 6, 1904, the new two-story college building adjoining St. Paul's Station was dedicated. Its total cost was $4,007. Up to the year 1910 the institution had the same three departments which its sister college in Greensboro has. In that year, however, the Theological Department was closed, after it had graduated one theological candidate — Rev. Calvin Peter Thompson. The High School Department and the Normal Department were continued till the end of the school-year 1925, when the institution was

Alabama Luther College, Selma.
On the left, lecture halls and chapel;
on the right, the dormitory.

closed for two reasons: 1. Luther College no longer fulfilled the real purpose for which it was opened. 2. New buildings would have cost at least $18,500. In view of the fact that the funds needed for the dormitory in Greensboro were not coming in; and in view of the further fact that Synodical Conference had instructed the Board to establish an institution of higher learning in the promising Alabama field, it was deemed advisable to close Luther College.

ALABAMA LUTHER COLLEGE.

The rapid expansion of the Alabama Missions and the lack of teachers available for the Alabama schools necessitated the appointment of teachers who were not properly qualified. For this reason the Alabama Luther Conference, in 1919, petitioned the Synodical Conference for a high school normal. The following year Synodical Conference granted this petition, in-

The First Class of Alabama Luther College, March 1, 1923.

Seated (left to right): Mrs. Nettie Moore, teacher; Evie Dale, Mary Bodly, Carrie Gullett, Emma Dukes, Prof. Otho Lynn.

Standing (left to right): Julia Jenkins, Grace Smith, Gertrude McBryde, Fannie Ramsey, Carrie Stallworth, Irma Dulaney.

structing the Mission Board to establish the desired institution as soon as possible. Up to the convention in 1922 it had not been possible to carry out this resolution; but now it was resolved to carry out the former resolution without further delay. The beautiful city of Selma, on the Alabama River, was chosen as the future home of our baby college. In a rented

The Faculty of Alabama Luther College.
Seated: Mrs. Lou Jenkins, matron; Miss Anna Hudson.
Standing: Prof. P. D. Lehman; Prof. Otho Lynn, president; Prof. I. Holness.

cottage at 520 First Ave. the school was opened by Prof. R. O. L. Lynn on November 13, 1922. Nine Lutheran girls were enrolled the first year. Mrs. Nettie Moore assisted Professor Lynn, while Rosa Young acted as matron. Teaching began on the morning of November 16. The institution is a junior high school. A fifth year has been added for a normal department. The first four girls graduated June 1, 1926: Gertrude McBryde, Carrie G. Stallworth, Lela M. Young, and Grace H. Smith.

NEW COLLEGE BUILDINGS.

In the spring of 1925 the Mission Board bought thirteen acres of land in the northeastern part of Selma for $12,300. There was a small cottage on the ground. The dormitory and recitation hall, which were erected during the summer of 1925, cost about $36,000. They were dedicated on Sunday afternoon, September 20, 1925. The writer had the pleasure of delivering the dedicatory sermon. In September, 1925, an elementary school was erected on the campus at a cost of $2,700. This school is attended by the children of the neighborhood and also by such students as are not sufficiently prepared to enter the high school.

The faculty of Alabama Luther College is composed of Professor and President R. O. L. Lynn, Prof. Paul D. Lehman, Prof. Isaac Holness, and Miss Anna J. Hudson. Mrs. Lou Jenkins is the present matron. In agreement with a resolution adopted by the Mission Board at the plenary meeting held April 21, 1922, the faculty consists exclusively of colored persons. Another feature is to be found in the fact that the entire student-body is composed of members of the Lutheran Church. The school is a girls' school and aims to educate and train future teachers for our mission-schools; however, as long as there is room, boys who purpose to prepare for the ministry may attend. They occupy the five-room cottage.

THE CHARACTER OF OUR COLORED PASTORS.

Having attended our high school four years and our theological seminary three years, our pastors have become thoroughly acquainted with Lutheran doctrine and cultus and are qualified to teach others. The writer said in his 1916 report to the Synodical Conference: —

"We are sometimes asked, What satisfaction do our colored pastors give? The answer to this question, in general, is favorable. Their congregations testify that they render faithful service and set a good example to them and their children. For this reason, as well as because of the good education they have received, they enjoy the respect of such colored people as are without and even of the better class of whites. Of course, together with their people they must suffer, more or less, from race prejudice." I made this statement eleven years ago. During these eleven years I have not been obliged to revise this favorable opinion. Our colored pastors have my confidence and good will. But perhaps it will be best to let an outsider speak.

A pastor of the North Carolina Synod says in the *Lutheran* (October 21, 1920, p. 14): "Two years ago I looked in upon a Negro graduate of the college and seminary at Greensboro, doing pastoral work in the community in which I was reared. I found him intelligent and a well-versed defender of our cultus and faith. His church was neat and all its furniture Lutheran in arrangement and design. On inquiry from neighbors in my home community I learned that conversions are genuine and that a different character is animating that particular settlement now from that which had moved it twenty-five years ago."

God be praised and thanked for having graciously given us a pious colored ministry! May He ever adorn them with purity of doctrine and with the beauty of holiness!

XIII. "A Peculiar People, Zealous of Good Works."

Christ came into the world to save sinners and to sanctify those who believe in Him. "He gave Himself for us that He might redeem us from all iniquity and purify unto Himself a peculiar people" (a people for His own possession). Salvation and sanctification are also the aim and end of all missionary endeavors.

How about the sanctification, or the holiness of life, of our colored Lutherans? The writer does not wish to create a false impression. It is not his intention to paint a paradise in which there is no sin and no temptation to sin. Even as in our white congregations, so also in our colored congregations there is no perfection, but much weakness. And so our missionaries meet with all kinds of disappointments and sad experiences. They stand in need of patience and perseverance. And yet, looking at it with the eyes of faith, we see in our colored Lutheran Church a beautiful garden, where the heavenly Gardener produces flowers and fruits of holiness. Here again we shall let others speak.

Rev. Westcott, of Selma, Ala., received this unasked-for testimonial from a white lady: "It gives me pleasure to say that I believe N. N. a good, consistent, Christian woman. She has been with me for more than a year and is faithful, conscientious, and helpful. She gives me much confidence in the good teachings and usefulness of the Church she represents. Her Church is fortunate in sending out members of such high standard."

Mr. W. H. Wilson, tax assessor and collector of Autauga County, Alabama, said to our Pastor Weeke several years ago: "The only good Negroes around here are the Lutheran Negroes. They have less debts, pay their bills more regularly, are more thrifty, and their morality is better than that of any of the rest around here."

The owner of a grocery in Kannapolis, N. C., had this to say to a crowd of men in his place of business: "I want to tell you, men, I haven't got much to say about these colored churches around here; half of them are doing no good. But there is one colored church I would place ahead of all colored churches and equal with a whole lot of these white churches, and that is that Lutheran church over there in Texas." Texas is the name of the neighborhood where our Mount Calvary Church stands.

Mr. Charles Cook, of Concord, who has had extensive business dealings with colored people, once said to the writer: "If all the Negroes would be like your Lutheran Negroes, they would be all right."

A white pastor of the South, not a member of the Synodical Conference, wrote in a Southern church-paper: "Many of our people will tell you that the Lutheran Negroes, taking them all round, are the best we have."

Prof. J. Horine, of Columbia, S. C., has made this strong statement: "It is the rule that the colored Lutherans are as intelligent and worshipful, as loyal and liberal, as orthodox and moral, as any white Lutherans to be found anywhere."

We thank God for this fine reputation which our colored Lutheran fellow-Christians enjoy among their fellow-citizens.

A REMARKABLE DEATH-RATE.

According to the census of 1920 the death-rate among the colored people of this country was 18 per thousand in that year. In our colored Lutheran Church, however, the death-rate was only 9 per thousand. This surprisingly low death-rate is an evidence of the complete change of heart and life experienced by the colored people when they become real Lutherans. Such persons are completely changed, leading an altogether different life. God fulfils His promise for them, the promise "that it may be well with thee and thou mayest *live long* on the earth." Yes, it pays to be a real Lutheran.

ORDERLY SERVICES.

People who only know of the loud and disorderly meetings of the sectarian Negroes can scarcely imagine how quiet and orderly the church services of our colored Lutherans are. A member of a white Lutheran church, having visited one of our colored Lutheran churches, exclaimed in surprise: "Why, these colored people in our Mission are just as quiet and well-behaved as the people in our German congregations, as I have just now seen in your church." People at first imagined that a Church which is as quiet as our Lutheran Church would have no success among the colored people; but their opinion has certainly been disproved by the growth of our missions.

CONTRIBUTIONS.

Giving for the work of the Church is a pretty good barometer of spiritual life. This barometer shows that there is real spiritual life in our colored Lutheran congregations. Of course, some members are slackers and need admonition and exhortation, as is the case everywhere, without respect to color or condition.

It is generally known that the colored man is poor, very

Robt. Dixon, New Orleans.
Polly Rowlett, Meherrin.

poor, as a rule. But as the widow in the gospel gave her mite, so does the colored Christian. It has happened that a poor colored woman has sold her last hen on Saturday in order that she might lay her offering on the contribution-plate on Sunday. It is most gratifying to see how our colored brethren and sisters are growing in the grace of giving for the kingdom of God from year to year. In 1916 the total of contributions received from the mission-field was $6,500; but after ten years, by 1926, the contributions exceeded $32,600. This represents an increase of more than $26,000 in the last ten years. The contributions of our white Lutherans have increased very much in these ten years; but the increase does not nearly approximate that of our colored Lutherans. What does this increase in contributions prove? It plainly proves that our colored fellow-Lutherans are rapidly and in a remarkable degree learning to help themselves. We have heard of Ellen Bransford and Leah Jones in Little Rock, who gave their all to the Lord and His Church. Other instances

Jim McBride and Emily Bridges.
Two old members at Rosebud, Ala.

of cheerful and liberal giving might be enumerated if space would permit.

Though our colored fellow-Christians have made fine progress in the grace of giving, they by no means feel that they may now stand still and rest on their laurels. They are anxious to do more. May God grant them the ability to carry out their good and praiseworthy intentions!

GUESTS AT THE LORD'S TABLE.

Our blessed Lord and Savior wants His Christians to partake of His Holy Supper frequently. Luther says in his preface to the Smaller Catechism: "If a person does not seek nor desire the Lord's Supper at least some four times a year, it is to be feared that he despises the Sacrament and is not a Christian, just as he is not a Christian who refuses to believe or to hear the Gospel."

How often do the confirmed members of our white congregations partake of the Lord's Supper on an average during the year? The average is about two; in our colored congregations the average is more than three. In several of our colored congregations the confirmed members commune five times and even six times a year. By thus having their faith in the forgiveness of their sins frequently strengthened, they receive strength to struggle against, and overcome, the enemies of their soul and to walk in godliness and good works.

Four Generations of Lutherans.
Atlanta, Ga.

INDOCTRINATION OF OUR MEMBERS.

The Lutheran Church is a teaching Church. Christ's parting command was: "Teach them." As a result of her teaching activity her members are intelligent; they know what they believe; they know what their Church stands for. This is true also of our colored Lutheran members. They are indoctrinated in church, school, Sunday-school, and in the catechumen class.

Besides the foregoing the printed page is employed as

a means of indoctrination. Forty-nine years ago the Synodical Conference issued the *Lutheran Pioneer*. This paper has entered the homes of our people for nearly half a century. Rev. F. J. Lankenau has edited the *Pioneer* since the beginning of 1913. The paper appears once a month, bringing sixteen pages of reading-matter and pictures. The subscription price is 50 cents a year.

In June, 1921, our Alabama workers began to publish the *Alabama Lutheran*. At its convention in 1922 the Synodical Conference resolved that this new publication should be used in the entire Mission. Accordingly, the name was changed, in 1923, to the *Colored Lutheran*. Superintendent Geo. Schmidt

Two Little Lutherans, Rockwell, N. C.

is the editor. The paper appears once a month and costs 50 cents a year. Each congregation orders a sufficient number of copies for every family, as also for other free distribution.

STEADFASTNESS OF OUR COLORED LUTHERANS.

Are the colored people who join our Church faithful and steadfast? This question is often put, and generally in a tone of doubt. What is the truth in the matter? Sad to say, we have to admit that not all who promise faithfulness at the altar when they are confirmed remain true to their solemn vow. But after all, our experience with colored members is probably no worse than it is with white members. The workers in our Colored Missions can tell many an encouraging thing concerning the steadfastness and loyalty of their members. The writer once heard Rev. Ed H. Schmidt make the following statement before a gathering of colored people at a new mission-station: "I am the pastor of a colored congregation numbering almost 400 baptized members. If some one should go to my people and point a loaded pistol at them, saying, 'You must quit the Lutheran Church or I'll shoot,' they would say, 'Shoot!' "

LOCKED UP IN A DARK ROOM.

In St. Paul's, New Orleans, there was a seventeen-year-old girl of whom one of the former missionaries tells this touching story: —

For years this girl had been made fun of by near relatives and members of her own house because of her Lutheranism. From early till late they heaped derision and contempt upon her. At the instigation of a Methodist preacher she was dragged into his church and to the mourners' bench. But she declared: "You can force me and drag me to the mourners' bench, but you cannot force me to give up my faith and deny my Savior." Now they tried another scheme: They locked her up eight days in a dark room. For almost a whole week the "sisters" and the preacher tried their hand at perverting her. When her pastor got to see her one day, she stood there with sunken cheeks, expressionless eyes, on the brink of despair. He prayed with her and comforted her with passages from Holy Writ, and she was strengthened again. The following Sunday the girl went, not, as expected, to the Methodist church, but to the Lutheran chapel. By her steadfastness and faithfulness she finally led her father and mother to come over to the Lutheran Church. May God grant us such loyalty!

Let me be Thine forever,
Thou faithful God and Lord;
Let me forsake Thee never
Nor wander from Thy Word;
Lord, do not let me waver,
But give me steadfastness,
And for such grace forever
Thy holy name I'll bless.

XIV. Brief Biographies of Our White Pastors and Professors.

1. *Prof. Walter Herman Beck.* Born November 7, 1898, in Milwaukee. Graduated from the seminary at Wauwatosa, Wis., in June, 1922. He is the first missionary furnished by the Wisconsin Synod. Rev. Wm. Schink was the second. Candidate Beck was ordained and installed in Mount Zion, New Orleans, September 8, 1922, and served till the summer of 1925,

when he was called as professor to Immanuel Lutheran College in Greensboro. Since September, 1926, he also serves the congregation at High Point.

2. *Prof. Frederick Berg.* Born March 20, 1856. Graduated from the St. Louis Seminary shortly before Easter, 1878. Ordained by Rev. C. F. Obermeyer in June, 1878. Berg was our first resident missionary in Little Rock. At the end of October, 1881, he accepted a call to Indiana. About ten years later he followed a call to St. John's in Beardstown, Ill. In 1911 our Board called him as professor and president of Immanuel Lutheran

Rev. C. F. Drewes,
Director of Missions.

College. He arrived in Greensboro June 30, 1911. Berg served as president of the institution till the summer of 1919. He teaches in the Theological Department exclusively and is one of the ablest Lutheran theologians in the United States. If God grants him another year on this earth, he will be able to celebrate his golden jubilee.

3. *Rev. Lawrence G. Dorpat.* Born April 8, 1862, at Strawberry Point, Iowa. His mother was sent to America by Loehe as one of the first deaconesses. He graduated from the Springfield Seminary in 1883 and was minister in Wisconsin till the fall of 1920. He was installed at Meherrin November 21, 1920. He also teaches school.

4. *Rev. Martin Dorpat,* a son of the foregoing. Born January 7, 1899,

near Sheboygan, Wis. Graduated from the Springfield Seminary in June, 1926. Ordained and installed June 20, 1926, in St. Matthew's, Meherrin. He serves as assistant missionary at Meherrin and as traveling missionary in Virginia and North Carolina.

5. *Director Christopher F. Drewes.* Born January 12, 1870, at Wolcottsville, Niagara County, N. Y. Attended Concordia College at Fort Wayne from 1883 to 1889. Graduated from the St. Louis Seminary in June, 1892. Was pastor of Trinity in Memphis, Tenn., from July 5, 1892, to October, 1894, pastor of St. John's at Hannibal, Mo., from November 11, 1894, to October 16, 1905, pastor of Bethany in St. Louis from October 16, 1905, to

Rev. G. Kreft, Mobile.

April 30, 1917. A member of the Board for Colored Missions since August, 1908; chairman of the Board from September 15, 1911, to 1916; Director of Missions since May 1, 1917; editor of the *Missionstaube* since September 15, 1911; also author of an explanation of Luther's Small Catechism in questions and answers. During the ten years of his directorship he has had the pleasure of seeing the Lord cause our Colored Missions to grow from about 2,300 souls to about 5,200 and the contributions to increase from about $6,500 to more than $32,600 a year.

6. *Rev. Paul Edgar Gose.* Born February 25, 1896, at Grant Park, Ill. Taught in our mission-school in St. Louis 1918 to 1921, at Immanuel Lutheran College 1921 to 1923. Graduated from the St. Louis Seminary June 9, 1925. Installed as pastor of Grace Church, St. Louis, June 14, 1925.

7. *Rev. Melvin Holsten.* Born July 26, 1898, at Concordia, Mo. Taught in Bethlehem and Mount Zion, New Orleans, 1918 to 1920.

Graduated from the St. Louis Seminary in June, 1923. Ordained and installed at Concord, N. C., September 16, 1923. He also serves Immanuel at Shankletown, a suburb of Concord.

8. *Prof. William H. Kampschmidt.* Born April 17, 1894, in St. Louis. In 1907, he was confirmed by the writer. Graduated from Concordia Seminary in St. Louis in 1917. Pastor at Roseau and at Wadena, Minn., until called to Immanuel Lutheran College in Greensboro, where he arrived in August, 1924.

9. *Rev. Geo. Kase.* Born July 12, 1879, in Huntington, Ind. Graduated from the St. Louis Seminary. Began to serve Immanuel in Cincinnati in August, 1922. He is also city and institutional missionary.

10. *Superintendent G. M. Kramer.* See the brief biography on page 82.

11. *Rev. Gustave G. Kreft.* Born August 2, 1900, at New Minden, Ill. Did supply-work in Alabama 1922 and 1923. Graduated from the St. Louis Seminary June 9, 1925. Serves the stations in Mobile, Atmore, and Pensacola.

12. *Prof. Frank C. Lankenau.* Born March 13, 1897, in New Orleans, where his father, F. J. Lankenau, was missionary for seventeen years. Taught in Mount Zion and Luther College 1918 to 1919. Graduated from the St. Louis Seminary, June 9, 1921. In the fall of that year he began to teach in Immanuel.

13. *Rev. Oscar William Luecke.* Born May 5, 1890, in St. Genevieve, Mo. Graduated from the St. Louis Seminary in June, 1915. Was pastor at Abita Springs, La., and superintendent of Bethlehem Orphans' Home in New Orleans. Professor and president of Luther College from December, 1924, until the institution was closed in 1925. Pastor of Mount Zion in New Orleans, since September 3, 1925.

14. *Prof. Hans Naether.* Born February 7, 1886, at Torgau, Germany. Was baptized in the church where Luther's wife lies buried. Called to our Greensboro College in the fall of 1923. He also serves Luther Memorial and the station at Pomona.

15. *Prof. Henry Nau, Ph. D.* Born September 21, 1881, in Hesse-Nassau. Graduated from the St. Louis Seminary in 1905. Was missionary in India. Called to Luther College in March, 1921, and transferred to Immanuel Lutheran College in Greensboro in June, 1925. He is professor and president of the institution.

16. *Superintendent George A. Schmidt.* See page 65.

17. *Rev. Andrew Schulze.* Born March 8, 1896, in Cincinnati. Was in the United States Navy during the late war. Graduated from the Springfield Seminary in June, 1924. Installed as pastor of Holy Trinity in Springfield, August 17, 1924. He also serves the Jacksonville station.

18. *Rev. Paul Trumpoldt.* Born at Philadelphia, February 17, 1900. Graduated from Concordia Seminary, St. Louis, June 5, 1924. Pastor of St. Philip's, Philadelphia, since August 3, 1924.

19. *Rev. J. E. Shufelt.* Born November 8, 1888, in Town of Ghent, N. Y. Graduated from Hartwick Seminary June 26, 1918. Entered the service of our Colored Missions in August, 1921, as professor in Greensboro. Pastor of our churches at Bostian Cross Roads, Rockwell, and Gold Hill, N. C., since January 1, 1924.

20. *Rev. Paul John George Weeke.* Born March 21, 1891, at St. Louis. Graduated from the Springfield Seminary, in June, 1917. Pastor at Morrison, Ill., and Superior, Wis. Missionary at Joffre and Holy Ark, since March 2, 1924.

21. *Rev. Edward August Westcott.* Born January 3, 1895, at Boston. Graduated from the Springfield Seminary in June, 1920. Ordained and installed in Alabama, October 17, 1920. Has served various congregations in Alabama; has also served as acting superintendent.

22. *Rev. Erich Herbert Wildgrube.* Born March 5, 1896, at Bialystock, Russia. Graduated from the St. Louis Seminary in 1919. Was pastor at Renault, Ill. Installed at St. Paul's, New Orleans, March 5, 1922.

Superintendent F. D. Alston,
Charlotte, N. C.

COLORED PASTORS AND PROFESSORS.

1. *Superintendent Frank D. Alston.* Born December 4, 1886, in Raleigh, N. C. Graduated from Immanuel Lutheran College as teacher in 1907. Was teacher in Greensboro and Charlotte. Graduated from the same institution as pastor in May, 1915. Was pastor at Spartanburg, S. C., Salisbury, Drys Schoolhouse, Mount Pleasant, N. C., and is still in charge of Mount Calvary near Kannapolis, N. C. Was appointed superintendent of the eight colored pastors and their stations in the Southeastern Field in 1926.

2. *Rev. Isaac John Alston.* Born August 14, 1883, at Raleigh, N. C. Spent one term at Martin Luther College in New Ulm, Minn. Studied in Springfield, 1902. Finished his theological studies in Greensboro, June, 1909. He served the stations at Mount Pleasant, Drys Schoolhouse, Reimerstown, and Miller's Station, all in Cabarrus Co., N. C. Pastor in Atlanta since January 1, 1918.

3. *Rev. Eugene R. Berger.* Born July 30, 1887, near Mansura, La. Graduated from Immanuel, June 3, 1911. Has been pastor in Napoleonville, La., in Alabama, and since October 14, 1924, at Alexandria, La.

4. *Rev. Walter F. Carlson.* Born April 15, 1898. Studied in Greensboro. Has been pastor in Greenville, N. C., and in Alabama. He is in charge of the station at Tinela since July, 1923, and of the stations at Oak Hill, Rosebud, and Hamburg, Ala., since October, 1926.

5. *Rev. Marmaduke Nathanael Carter.* Born March 7, 1881, in Hanover Co., Va. Studied at Capital University, Columbus, O., and at the Teachers' Training-school of Baltimore. Studied theology privately and was ordained in May, 1917. Was transferred to Alabama, where he arrived

October 21, 1916. Served the stations at Rosebud and Possum Bend, Ala. Was sent on a lecture tour in September, 1921. Has been in charge of St. Philip's, Chicago, since March 2, 1924.

6. *Rev. Eugene B. Cozart.* Graduated from Immanuel Lutheran College in 1922. Served the stations at Joffre and Selma, Ala., from August 6, 1922, to March 2, 1924. Taught a term at Alabama Luther College. In charge of the stations at Vredenburgh and Buena Vista, Ala., since the fall of 1924 and of the station at Longmile, Ala., since October, 1926.

7. *Rev. William Eddleman.* Born at Bostian Cross Roads, N. C. Graduated from Immanuel Lutheran College in May, 1925. In charge of Pilgrim, Birmingham, since October 4, 1925.

8. *Rev. Fred Hiram Foard.* Born August 9, 1877, at Concord, N. C. Confirmed by Rev. David J. Koonts. Graduated from Immanuel Lutheran College in 1909. Has served the stations at Gold Hill, Rockwell, Bostian Cross Roads, Albemarle, High Point, and Southern Pines, N. C. In charge of the stations at Monroe, Drys Schoolhouse, and Mount Pleasant since September 14, 1926.

Rev. M. N. Carter,
Chicago.

9. *Rev. John W. Fuller.* Born December 9, 1881, at Apex, N. C. Attended Shaw University at Raleigh, N. C. Graduated from Immanuel Lutheran College June 1, 1917. Pastor at Meherrin, Va., July 1, 1917, to November 21, 1920; Spartanburg, S. C., November 21, 1920, to August, 1925. In charge of the three stations in Charlotte, N. C., since August, 1925.

10. *Rev. William Otto Hill.* Born December 2, 1889, at Yanceyville, N. C. Graduated from Immanuel Lutheran College in June, 1910. Taught school in Charlotte from June 3, 1910, to February 27, 1911. Received the call to Bethany, Yonkers, N. Y., February 27, 1911, and arrived there March 9, 1911.

11. *Prof. Isaac Holness.* Born 1890. Ordained and installed in Pilgrim, Birmingham, in March, 1923. Has taught in Alabama Luther College since September, 1925.

12. *Rev. Jesse A. Hunt.* Born November 12, 1889, in Silver Hill Township, Davidson Co., N. C. Graduated from Immanuel Lutheran College in May, 1918. Was ordained and installed August 25, 1918, in St. James's, Southern Pines. In charge of St. Mark's, Winston-Salem, since February 12, 1921.

13. *Rev. Wiley H. Lash.* Born near Greensboro, N. C. Was confirmed by Rev. J. C. Schmidt and sent to the Springfield Seminary by him.

Graduated in 1904. Has been pastor at Salisbury, Catawba, Conover, etc. Pastor of Grace, Greensboro, and Trinity, Elon College, since October, 1923.

14. *Prof. Paul D. Lehman.* Born October 12, 1896, near Mansura, La. A graduate of Immanuel Lutheran College. Ordained and installed at Wilmington, N. C., May 30, 1918. Was transferred to Bethel, Charlotte, N. C., August 12, 1918, to Alabama Luther College, June 10, 1923. He also serves Trinity Congregation at Selma.

15. *Prof. Robert Otho L. Lynn.* Born June 24, 1891, at Mount Pleasant, N. C. Graduated from Immanuel Lutheran College in 1912. Was pastor at Greensboro, Elon College, High Point, and Winston-Salem, N. C. Arrived in Alabama October 21, 1916, and served congregations at Vredenburgh, Buena Vista, and Tinela. Served in the United States Army in

Some of Our Pastors. 1925.

Seated, left to right: Rev. F. D. Alston, Rev. M. N. Carter, Rev. J. McDavid, Rev. W. Lash, Rev. C. D. Peay.
Standing: Rev. C. March, Rev. Wm. Hill, Rev. J. W. Fuller, Rev. G. Roberts, Rev. Jesse Hunt.

France during the World War. Professor and president of Alabama Luther College since November, 1922. He also serves the station at Kings Landing.

16. *Rev. John McDavid.* Born January 4, 1878, in Macon, Miss. Entered Concordia at Springfield September 5, 1892. Taught school in Holy Trinity at Springfield from 1897 to 1904. Opened a mission-school in St. Louis November 16, 1904, and gathered and instructed the first confirmation class in St. Louis. Was sent to Charlotte, where he was ordained and installed July 23, 1905. He has at various times served congregations in Monroe, Southern Pines, High Point, N. C., in Spartanburg, S. C., and in Atlanta. Was transferred to Los Angeles, Cal., in 1925, and installed in Los Angeles, September 13, 1925.

17. *Rev. Carrington R. March.* Born November 13, 1888. Graduated from the Greensboro Seminary June 1, 1911. He has served congregations

at Southern Pines, Fayetteville, Mount Pleasant, and Gold Hill. Has been pastor at Salisbury since July 1, 1923. He also serves the stations at Catawba and Conover.

18. *Rev. James Samuel Montgomery.* Born October 18, 1882, in Alabama. He has been pastor of Bethany, Nyland, Ala., since September 11, 1921. He also serves the stations at Pine Hill, Arlington, and Lamison.

19. *Rev. Wilfred J. Tervalon.* Born August 6, 1893, in New Orleans. Graduated from the Greensboro Seminary in 1914 and has served congregations at Richmond, Va., Mansura, La., and is pastor at Napoleonville, La., since August, 1925. He also teaches school.

20. *Rev. Charles D. Peay.* Born September 21, 1888, at Concord, N. C. Graduated from the Greensboro Seminary in 1909. He has been pastor at Monroe and Southern Pines, N. C., Mansura and New Orleans, La., at various places in Alabama, and has been in charge of the congregations at Camden, Possum Bend, Rockwest, and Midway, since October, 1926.

21. *Rev. Calvin Peter Thompson.* Born June 11, 1883, near Mansura, La. Was the first and only theological graduate of Luther College. He was ordained July 17, 1910, and sent to Merigold in Sunflower Co., Miss., July 21, 1910; thence to Bethlehem School in New Orleans, thence to Charlotte, N. C., where he served Bethel Congregation; he also served the station at Monroe. Owing to ill health he was at his home in Mansura for about a year. Installed in Napoleonville, La., in August, 1917, in Mansura in August, 1925. He also teaches school.

22. *Rev. John Thompson.* Born May 3, 1886, near Mansura, La. Graduated from the normal department in Greensboro in 1913. Taught in St. Paul's School, New Orleans, and Rosebud, Ala., since 1922. Studied theology privately and was ordained and installed at Tilden, Ala., August 2, 1925. He also serves the stations at Ingomar, Taits, and Ackerville.

XV. The Growth of Our Colored Missions.

Fifty years ago the little acorn was planted when Rev. Doescher was sent out as a prospector and traveled through six Southern States. The acorn germinated and sent forth a little shoot. Lack of sufficient missionary funds, numerous changes in the pastorates, as well as other hindrances kept it from growing rapidly during the first three decades. The opening of the North Carolina field in 1891, and particularly the opening of the field in the Black Belt of Alabama, in 1916, marked the beginning of comparatively rapid growth. To-day the acorn has grown to be a tree which spreads its branches over fourteen States of the Union: Alabama, Arkansas, California, Florida, Georgia, Illinois, Louisiana, Missouri, New York, North Carolina, South Carolina, Ohio, Pennsylvania, and Virginia. We have not included Michigan, where Rev. Storm is doing work among the colored people near Free Soil, nor have we included in our statistics the missions conducted in Cleveland and Buffalo.

The Second General Conference, Held in Concord, N. C., 1925.

Front row, left to right: Rev. M. Holsten, Superintendent G. A. Schmidt, Prof. H. Naether, Rev. E. Wildgrube, Director C. F. Drewes, Prof. F. Berg, Rev. M. Carter, President Im. Albrecht, Superintendent J. Ph. Smith.

The Conference meets biennially.

THE GROWTH OF OUR MISSIONS BY DECADES.

BAPTIZED MEMBERS, OR SOULS.

1877	0	1907	1,908
1887	301	1917	2,900
1897	1,400	1926	5,123

These figures do not tell of the thousands of people who are favorably influenced by our work in church and school. It may be safely estimated that this number is approximately 25,000. By the blessing of God the missionary enterprise which was begun fifty years ago has been successful beyond expectation. To God be all the glory!

The wonderful growth which the good Lord has permitted our Colored Missions to experience during these fifty years shows that the money which our Christians have given for this missionary enterprise was money well spent.

Although our colored Lutheran Church has made remarkable progress during this half century, there is still much land to be possessed. We have but one mission-station each in Florida with its 330,000, in Arkansas with its 475,000, in Virginia with its 690,000, in South Carolina with its 865,000, and in Georgia with its 1,200,000 colored people. Just think of it, only five mission-stations among more than three million people! But that is not all. The 150,000 Negroes of Oklahoma, the 235,000 of Kentucky, the 240,000 of Texas, the 450,000 of Tennessee, and the 935,000 of Mississippi — more than two million people in five great States — have not a single Lutheran missionary in their midst. What a vast unoccupied field! True, many of these people belong to a church; however, the preachers of these churches are often blind leaders of the blind, not knowing even the abc of the Christian religion. To those who hear them the way of life remains hidden. Said old "Uncle" Simon: "Pastor, I was a member of the M. Church for forty years, but during all these years I never heard that Jesus died for my sins on the cross and that I shall be saved if I believe in Him. If the Lutheran Church had not come here, I should have been lost." Hundreds of thousands are still in the same sad plight in which "Uncle" Simon was. Their sad lot calls to us for pity and help.

Besides these nominal members of the Christian Church there are untold thousands who do not even outwardly belong to a church. These poor, perishing people are without God and without hope in the world. They know naught of the

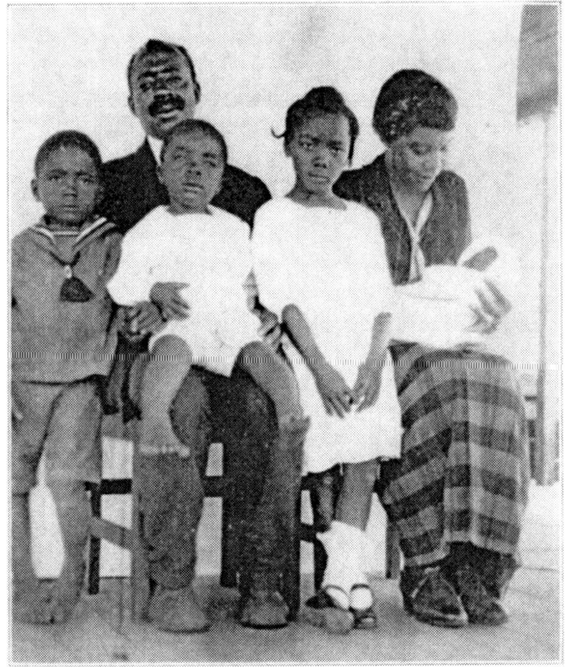

One of Our Missionaries and His Family.
Rev. F. Foard, Monroe, N. C.

love of God in Christ Jesus. Heedlessly they hurry along the broad way that leadeth to destruction. Can their temporal and eternal ruin leave us cold and unmoved? Should not the divine mercy which we have experienced lead us to rescue the perishing and bring the light of the Gospel of Jesus to those who sit in darkness and in the shadow of death?

Shall we, whose souls are lighted
With wisdom from on high, —
Shall we to men benighted
The lamp of life deny?

No, let us follow the example of Philip, who preached Jesus to the Ethiopian eunuch, and proclaim the precious, saving Gospel to the religiously neglected and forsaken Negroes, that they may be saved and glorify our Father who is in heaven.

May our kind heavenly Father be with our colored Lutheran Zion in the future as He has been with it in the past fifty years! May He graciously preserve unto her His holy Word in all its truth and purity and cause her to be the spiritual mother of thousands of ten thousands!

Philip and the Ethiopian Eunuch.
"And he preached to him Jesus." Acts 8, 35.

CPSIA information can be obtained
at www.ICGtesting.com
Printed in the USA
FSOW02n0955270617
35678FS